what's
your
grief?

what's your grief?

LISTS TO HELP YOU THROUGH ANY LOSS

Eleanor Haley, MS, and
Litsa Williams, MA, LCSW-C

QUIRK BOOKS

PHILADELPHIA

Library of Congress Cataloging-in-Publication Data
Names: Haley, Eleanor, author. | Williams, Litsa, author.
Title: What's your grief? : lists to help you through any type of loss
/ by Eleanor Haley and Litsa Williams.
Description: Philadelphia, PA : Quirk Books, [2022] | Includes bibliographical
references and index. | Summary: "A collection of lists intended to help readers
understand and cope with all forms of grief and loss"—Provided by publisher.
Identifiers: LCCN 2022003890 (print) | LCCN 2022003891 (ebook) |
ISBN 9781683693024 (hardcover) | ISBN 9781683693031 (ebook)
Subjects: LCSH: Grief—Psychological aspects. | Loss (Psychology)
Classification: LCC BF575.G7 H338 2022 (print) | LCC BF575.G7 (ebook) |
DDC 155.9/37—dc23/eng/20220214
LC record available at https://lccn.loc.gov/2022003890
LC ebook record available at https://lccn.loc.gov/2022003891

ISBN: 978-1-68369-302-4

Printed in China

Typeset in Greycliff and Recoleta

Designed by Andie Reid
Production management by John J. McGurk

Quirk Books
215 Church Street
Philadelphia, PA 19106
quirkbooks.com

10 9 8 7 6 5 4 3 2 1

Contents

Welcome to a Book
We Wish You Didn't Need

Dear Reader,

It's hard to welcome someone to a book like this. On the one hand, we wish you didn't need it. On the other hand, we're genuinely glad you're here.

As part-time skeptics, we tend to pick up books (especially self-help books) with caution. Though we don't want to assume that you're equally dubious, we'd still like to provide you with a little background about this book by answering a few key questions.

Why did we write this book?

As mental health professionals working in the field of grief and loss—and as people who've experienced grief ourselves—we've always seen it as our job to help people understand the vast range of emotions and experiences considered "normal" after loss. That's why we founded the online grief community What's Your Grief in late 2012. Since then, we've written hundreds of articles about grief and loss that are read by millions of grieving people and grief-support professionals each year.

We began writing this book in 2020. (And if you don't remember what happened in 2020, this book's life in print is far longer than we ever imagined.) That was a year of major change—of cancellations, quarantines, remote work, loss, loneliness, sickness, and death. It was a year in which everyone's eyes were open to the various shapes grief can take because everyone was experiencing loss on some scale. Still, many people also second-guessed their feelings and wondered, "Is it selfish to grieve things that seem minor when so many people are sick and dying?" Our simple answer to this question is no. Here's why:

> Though some losses may seem smaller than others, your losses are valid and worthy of recognition, no matter the size.

> There's no threshold one has to meet to feel grief-like things.

> One person's grief doesn't take away from another's.

Regardless of the type of loss you've experienced, only you know the extent of your pain and struggle. Your grief is a distinct and subjective experience influenced by many factors. Here are just a few:

> Grief is a reflection of you and your relationship with who or what has been lost.

> Loss often sets off a domino effect of subsequent losses. So you're likely grieving a web of interconnected losses.

> We all experience hardship, stress, and emotion differently. There is no one right way to grieve, there isn't a standard timeline, and there are many (many, many) ways to cope.

Thanks to myths and misconceptions about grief, people often assume it's formulaic. They think X type of loss will cause Y amounts of pain. Or they believe they'll simply go through grief's stages and come out on the other side. But grief isn't predictable or uniform; instead, it's highly variable and individual.

The individuality of grief makes it hard to understand, and people often feel thrown when their experience doesn't align with their expectation. It's common to wonder, "Is this normal, or am I losing it?" But most of the time, the answer to this question is, "Yes, you are normal." As the Holocaust survivor and psychiatrist Viktor Frankl wisely wrote in his 1946 book *Man's Search for Meaning,* "An abnormal reaction to an abnormal situation is normal behavior."

We can't save anyone from the messiness of grief, but hopefully we can help make it more manageable.

And in many ways, managing (rather than overcoming) grief is the goal. Or, if you prefer a different goal, you can choose tolerating it, integrating it, living with it, understanding it, maybe even growing from it if you're feeling ambitious. We know these goals lack a sense of closure compared to overcoming grief, but the truth is that this process is ongoing and most people don't just "get over it." This idea may be scary—but you will be okay, we promise.

Because as your relationship with grief evolves, you will likely also find hope and healing by changing how you respond to, cope with, and conceptualize grief. That's what we hope this book will help you do.

Why lists?

We've just established that grief is a complex human experience. So now you may be wondering where we got the nerve to approach something so complicated with something as simple as lists. Which we get.

Grief is intense and overwhelming enough as it is. It's always been our philosophy that people who are grieving shouldn't also be expected to trudge through dense and inaccessible grief support. The truth is, it makes the most sense to approach something as nuanced as grief one step at a time, whether that step is understanding a new concept, reflecting on an aspect of your loss, or learning about a new coping tool. So, our goal with these lists is to distill the most important information and share it with you in ways that are easy to understand and apply.

You should also understand that when we say *lists* we mean all sorts: to-do lists, not-to-do lists, informational lists, bucket lists, lists completed by us, and lists to be completed by you. We promise we'll never tell you your grief can be categorized or solved with a set of bullet points. We know your experience is unique, and the most meaningful answers you find are the ones you arrive at yourself.

Ultimately, we hope that you'll see this book as a place where you can begin to explore and understand your experiences related to loss and discover the ways to cope that work best for you.

How do you use this book?

When we began writing this book, it was tempting to approach it like a story, with a beginning, middle, and end. After all, there *is* an arc to grief, and wouldn't it feel reassuring to organize this confusing experience into such a familiar structure? Reassuring, yes, but accurate? Not entirely.

The truth is, grief stories rarely have an end and each is as different as books sitting on your shelf. We can't say things like, "First you'll feel this, then you'll feel that," because there are millions of different ways you might think, feel, and act in response to loss. We also can't say, "First comes the hurt and then comes the healing," because the reality is that you have to find ways to survive while the storm is still overhead.

In the end, we settled on three simple sections:

> 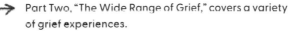 Part One, "The Basics of Grief," presents foundational information.

> 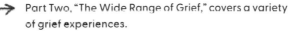 Part Two, "The Wide Range of Grief," covers a variety of grief experiences.

> 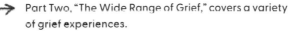 Part Three, "Coping with Grief," features concepts and ideas related to coping.

There's a general rationale for the order of these sections. However, if you were to put them up side by side, your grief experience would most likely look like a Ping-Pong ball bouncing back and forth among them.

We hope you choose to read the book all the way through. Though these lists may seem like independent topics unto themselves, they are often more interconnected than they appear. Some lists may not seem relevant to you right now, but grief is an ongoing experience. Concepts and ideas that don't resonate with you today may resonate later as your grief evolves, so it can't hurt to learn a little about them.

Now that we've made an appeal for reading the *whole* book, reading it linearly is not the only way to use it. You may want to pick and choose the lists that feel most personally relevant first. Maybe some lists don't seem to apply to your experience, or perhaps they present topics you don't feel ready to tackle. If you want to skip around, have at it! Above all else, we want you to use this book in a way that makes sense to you.

Here are a few more tips:

→ If you read any section in full, make it "The Basics of Grief." This section presents a lot of foundational information that's generally relevant regardless of your specific loss and experience.

→ Pay attention to the Other Lists to Check Out. After each list, we mention other related lists—which will help you find connected ideas, concepts, and coping tools.

→ Take it slow, and pause when you feel the need. This book covers a wide range of topics. Some might touch on places of deep personal pain. When that is the case, allow yourself plenty of time to process the section and to decompress afterward.

→ If you're the kind of person who likes seeing the full lay of the land before you start reading a book, check out the complete list of lists on page 294.

→ Try the **Make Your Own** lists. We want you to feel like you understand your own ongoing grief story more by the end of this book. The Make Your Own lists will help you reflect on your experiences as they relate to loss, grief, and your coping strengths and preferences.

→ Last but not least, we encourage you to keep an open mind about ideas that don't immediately seem like your thing. Grief challenges us in new ways, which sometimes means finding new and different ways to deal with it.

what's your grief?

1 Thing This Book Won't Do

Before getting started, we need to be upfront about one thing this book *won't* do. This book won't help you go back to being the person you were before experiencing loss.

People often think that grief is only about dealing with one primary loss—and of course, that's a big part of it. But grief is also about grieving for *yourself* because loss changes you, and it changes your world. Loss is like a tornado that touches down right in the middle of your life, shattering everything in its path into pieces so small there's no way you can put them back together.

Some losses have a more significant impact than other losses, of course. But even small losses can cause upheaval to your sense of self and your worldview, as your beliefs and assumptions about things like safety, trust, purpose, and meaning shift.

Though the tornado of loss may have left a trail of damage, it didn't destroy everything. And the things that are most likely to withstand strong winds are those that are firmly planted within *you*—things like your core values, principles, deeply held beliefs, and close relationships (much more on relationships later in the book). These are the things that will provide you with a foundation for living in a world that *has* to change.

One thing this book *will* do is help you solidify that foundation.

PART ONE

The Basics of Grief

Grief myths and misconceptions are a bit of a sore spot for us. They wreak havoc on grieving people and, therefore, need to be addressed early and often. If we do our job, by the end of this book you should be able to spot a grief myth from a mile away.

With that in mind, let's test your current grief-myth radar with the following true or false quiz. You don't have to keep track of your answers. No one is being graded; just mentally take note.

True or False?

1. GRIEF IS ALWAYS ASSOCIATED WITH DEATH.

2. GRIEF FOLLOWS A SET OF STAGES.

3. TIME HEALS ALL WOUNDS.

4. GRIEF IS ALL NEGATIVE FEELINGS.

5. GRIEF ENDS WITH ACCEPTANCE.

6. HEALTHY GRIEF MEANS GETTING OVER YOUR LOSS AND MOVING ON.

7. THE FIRST YEAR AFTER A LOSS IS ALWAYS THE HARDEST.

8. MOST PEOPLE FEEL BACK TO NORMAL AFTER A FEW WEEKS.

9. IF SOMEONE OR SOMETHING WAS BAD FOR YOU, THERE'S NO REASON TO GRIEVE THE LOSS OF IT.

10. PEOPLE SHOULD ONLY SEEK HELP AS A LAST RESORT FOR COPING WITH GRIEF.

If you answered **False** to all these statements, congratulations, you get 100 percent. If you said **True** to any of them, we promise you, you're not alone. If we're being honest, most of us come to grief believing some of these myths because until you experience it yourself, you can only assume how grief will be.

Your assumptions about loss and grief are shaped from an early age by influences such as society, cultural groups, religion, family attitudes, past experiences, television, books, movies, and other media. These influences may contain valuable insights, but each carries with it a significant margin of error when it comes to the realities of grief. Though it's tempting to feel bitter about misrepresentations of the grief experience, it seems unlikely that we have been intentionally deceived. Quite often misconceptions arise from a desire to understand, control, manage, and master grief. Misguided as this may be, it's a hopeful desire, not a malicious one.

Still, the impact of these myths is frustrating. Ultimately, they don't make things easier; they make things exponentially harder by creating false expectations and arbitrary rules around what, where, when, why, and how you can grieve. Myths and misconceptions create a distracting and unfair point of comparison. Many people find their experience deviates from what others dictate as normal and then worry they're doing grief wrong.

Learning about grief and loss is always a normalizing and helpful first step for people who are grieving. But we think it's especially important as you begin to explore more specific and personal grief experiences throughout this book and in other contexts of your life. The lists in Part One are meant to help you break down some of the barriers that have been created by misconceptions and to help you broaden your understanding of grief.

And if you came to this book with a wide lens already, these lists will hopefully fill in some details and create a more nuanced picture of life after loss.

5

Little-Known Truths About Grief

It's revealing that there are many more misconceptions about grief than there are truths. This tells us that it's frightening to face such an overwhelming experience without certainty—and that people crave the sense of control that knowing what to expect provides. But very few things are universal in grief—aside from the fact that we'll all experience it at some point.

The urge to categorize and predict often gets us into trouble because we wind up placing unnecessary boundaries around what people should grieve and how they should grieve it. The following list of truths pushes against these boundaries and, in doing so, dispels many existing myths about grief.

As broad as the following list may be, we hope reading it helps to normalize the wide range of thoughts, emotions, and responses you may be having in the days, months, and even years since experiencing loss.

(1)

You can grieve the loss of anything significant to you.

As we'll say time and again, there are many types of losses capable of evoking a grief response. These responses vary from person to person and differ in duration, depth, and complexity. It's important to know this because, often, people experience nondeath losses and feel they shouldn't be grieving or that they aren't deserving of grief support.

(2)

Grief is not a predictable process with a set timeline and an endpoint.

Probably the most common misconception about grief is that it follows a predictable course and timeline. But grief is not a uniform process; it doesn't follow a set of stages or phases, and it doesn't reach a fixed point of closure, recovery, or conclusion.

In grief, feelings, setbacks, breakthroughs, roadblocks, triggers, and resolutions can occur at unexpected times and for unpredictable durations. Living with grief is much like trying to swim past the break in the ocean— you wade in, but every once in a while, a wave comes up and knocks you back a few feet. You're still deeper than when you started, but not as deep as you were before the wave hit.

Once grief has occupied space in your life, it never entirely leaves. It may sit silently at times, but it's always there because it's connected to something significant that's had a lasting impact on your life. When a person is early on in their grief, the prospect of always grieving may be discouraging. But don't despair; when we say you will always grieve, we don't mean the dark and desperate days will last forever.

Grieving is about adapting to your losses and integrating your experiences into your life. Intense grief emotions should become more manageable as time goes on and you find new ways to cope with your losses. At the same time, you may find new sources of comfort, like fostering a continued bond with a loved one who died or finding meaning and purpose from nondeath losses.

(3)

No two people grieve in exactly the same way.

Grief is a universal human experience, and yet it's always different from person to person. Even people suffering the same loss will be affected differently—for example, siblings grieving the death of a parent or two people laid off from a job at the same time.

How you view your past, present, and future as related to your loss depends on many factors. Of primary significance is the space that whatever or whoever you lost occupied in your life. But almost as important are the unique ways that you cope with hardship and loss. These are influenced by many different factors, including your specific needs, coping skills, support system, access to resources, grieving style, and history of trauma and loss, as well as the broader social and cultural context in which you're grieving.

(4)

Grief is multifaceted.

Many people believe that grief is exclusively sadness, or that it is an exclusively emotional experience. This common myth leaves people surprised by the many ways they perceive distress after a loss. In reality, grief impacts many dimensions of a person's life, including the physical, psychological, spiritual, interpersonal, and behavioral.

(5)

Coping with grief takes many shapes.

As people who work in grief support, we're aware of the go-to coping recommendations, such as journaling, reading books about grief, support groups, and grief counseling. Though these are great tools for many people, they won't work for everyone. There are many other creative and useful approaches that are rarely discussed.

Coping with grief requires a person to deal with many different thoughts, emotions, and stressors. You're not just looking for one single coping skill to get you through. Instead, you're putting together a coping toolbox to help you as your grief evolves. Ultimately, constructive coping encompasses anything that allows a person to process their grief-related thoughts, emotions, and memories. It also includes anything that helps them feel better, increases well-being, or gives them a break from their grief. The types of coping you choose are unique to your loss and personal preferences but could include things like:

- learning to cook the foods your mother used to make
- talking to a friend who "gets it"
- writing about the pain of divorce
- taking a break from caregiving and spending a weekend away with good friends
- volunteering or getting involved in advocacy to create change or help others experiencing loss

---

OTHER LISTS TO CHECK OUT:

6 Life Domains Impacted by Loss, page 48

Make Your Own List: What's Your Grief Style?, page 54

4 Questions to Ask Yourself About Your Coping Style, page 176

64

Things We Wish
We'd Known About Loss

This list was crowdsourced from the What's Your Grief online community.

1. Bad things don't just happen to other people.

2. No matter how prepared you think you are for loss and grief, you can never be *fully* prepared.

3. There is no such thing as closure.

4. There is no timeline for grieving. You can't rush it.

5. Grief doesn't follow a set of stages.

6. You will never go back to who you were before the loss. Grief changes you, and that's okay.

7. You can grieve what you never had—for example, hopes and dreams for the future.

8. Everyone grieves differently. Try not to compare yourself to others.

9. It's normal to feel guilt.

10. It's normal to feel anger.

11. It's normal to feel fear.

12. It's normal to feel numb.

13. It's normal to feel a hundred different things.

14. Grief is messy and confusing.

15. Grief makes you feel like you're losing it sometimes.

16. Grief can cause physical pain like head and body aches.

17. Grief can make it hard to concentrate and complete daily tasks.

18. It's okay to cry, and it's okay not to cry.

19. Time does not heal all wounds.

20. Grief can make you question your faith.

21. Religious faith can also be strengthened by loss.

22. Grief can make you question your life, your purpose, and your goals.

23. Sometimes it gets worse before it gets better.

24. Grief can make you feel selfish and entitled.

25. Grief can make you push people away.

26. Grief lasts a lot longer than sympathy does.

27. People may pressure you to move on too quickly.

28. Grief makes people uncomfortable, so you can expect to have a few awkward encounters.

29. When people offer support, accept it.

30. Some people don't know what to say or will say the wrong things, but this doesn't mean they don't care.

31. Sometimes grief makes you feel angry and annoyed at everyone.

32. People will give you advice; it's up to you whether or not you follow it.

33. Some people will tell you what you should and shouldn't feel. Feel free to ignore them.

34. You are the only one who can say how you should feel.

35. Crisis brings out the best and the worst in families.

36. Different grieving styles can create strain and confusion between family members and friends.

37. You may find comfort in very unexpected places.

38. You can't compare losses, though some may try.

39. Any loss you grieve is a valid loss, though people will sometimes make you feel otherwise.

40. Sometimes the people you thought would be there for you are not, and your biggest supporters are those you never expected.

41. It's okay to tell people when they're not being helpful.

42. As taxing as it seems, sometimes you have to help people help you.

43. You can't protect children from experiencing difficult emotions after loss. Instead, help them find ways to cope with their thoughts and feelings.

44. You may have a whole list of things you think you could have or should have done differently.

45. "Why?" and "What if . . . ?" are unanswerable. The trick is to figure out how to live without the answers.

46. If you find you're thinking about guilt and regret to the point that it is harmful or unproductive, it may be time to talk to someone about it.

47. It's not weak to get counseling.

48. Talking isn't the only way to process your emotions.

49. You will see reminders of your loss everywhere.

50. You will have days when you feel totally and completely alone, whether you are or not.

51. Grief can make you do stupid and impulsive things. If you regret these things later, cut yourself some slack.

52. Don't make big decisions simply because you feel really good or really bad on a particular day.

53. You may grieve your past and present, as well as the future you wish you'd had.

54. Significant life events, holidays, and milestones may become bittersweet.

55. Watch your alcohol consumption and other forms of negative coping. These things can spiral out of control quickly.

56. It's hard to go back to "regular" life after a loss, but the bills still need to be paid.

57. One loss doesn't necessarily make the next any easier. Each loss is different.

58. For many people, grief is cumulative. New losses bring up feelings about old losses.

59. Part of the grief process is getting to know yourself as a different person.

60. Once your eyes are opened to loss, you see it everywhere in the world.

61. Love, warmth, and happy memories live on and can continue to be felt toward someone or something gone.

62. It's okay to live and laugh while also grieving. You can feel two seemingly conflicting things at once.

63. Grief can make you a stronger person than you were before.

64. It does get better. Slower than you might like, but it does.

OTHER LISTS TO CHECK OUT:

5 Little-Known Truths About Grief, page 19

Make Your Own List: What Are Your Grief Emotions?, page 68

3 FAQs About Coping with Life After Loss, page 172

7

Types of Grief You Should Know (but Probably Don't)

By now you know that grief is our normal and natural response to loss, all sorts of loss. But even the word *grief* can be deceptive. It implies that it is a singular experience, an emotional monolith.

In reality, we not only grieve different types of loss, both death and nondeath, but we also experience different *types of grief*. Knowing that these exist is the first step in better understanding your grief.

These are some of the most common types. Note that they overlap with one another, so there's a good chance that you will experience more than one.

1 ANTICIPATORY GRIEF

If there is one type of grief that people are familiar with beyond regular old grief, it is usually anticipatory grief. This is a term that was coined by the psychiatrist Erich Lindemann in the 1940s to describe the grief that begins before a loss. It starts the moment you realize that loss is inevitable and on the (reasonably imminent) horizon. When your mind opens to the harsh reality that in the not-too-distant future a relationship is going to end, that you will have to sell your longtime home, or that a person is dying, you'll start to grieve aspects of the person or the loss. You begin grieving the future you assumed you would have, and you may start imagining what your life will look like or feel like after the loss. It is important to remember that anticipatory grief doesn't mean that you will grieve any less, or that it will necessarily be easier, when the loss happens.

2 AMBIGUOUS GRIEF

Ambiguous loss is grieving someone who is still alive. Yes, we can and do grieve people who are still alive. In fact, it is surprisingly common.

Pauline Boss, the mother of ambiguous grief, has been writing about and researching this concept since the 1970s. She describes two main categories of ambiguous loss.

Grieving someone who is physically present but psychologically absent

This happens when someone is still part of your daily life, but they have experienced a cognitive or psychological change. This change impacts their identity and, as a result, your relationship. They are still physically present, but you grieve the loss of the person they used to be and the relationship you used to have. Common examples of this are grieving someone with Alzheimer's or dementia, a substance use disorder, acute onset of mental illness, or a traumatic brain injury.

Though a slight variation of the above, Boss observes that whenever a person has an identity change and is still treated as the person they used to be, this can be ambiguous loss. This can happen when a person transitions from their birth-assigned gender, joins or leaves a religious group, is early in addiction recovery, or experiences a significant loss or trauma and is expected to go back to who they were before.

In this case, the reason you grieve a person is because they are no longer part of your day-to-day life. Their absence is a stressor because it means you don't know how they are doing and sometimes you don't know if or when you will see them again. You may find yourself thinking, wondering, and worrying about the person a lot, in ways that can sometimes feel consuming. Common examples are divorces or break-ups, family separations through the foster care system, military deployments, incarceration, estrangement, and immigration.

Though these types of losses can sound very different, what they share is their ambiguity. There is no clear endpoint. There is no way to fix or resolve the circumstances. Instead one must learn to live within the uncertainty and with the grief (Boss, 2006).

3 NONFINITE GRIEF

While we're on the topic of losses without clear endpoints, another important type is nonfinite loss. From childhood, people form ideas about how they think (and hope) their lives will turn out. People imagine, make choices for, and work toward the future they believe they want or need. But many things in life are out of one's control. When life doesn't match up with your expectations, you may experience what is known as *nonfinite grief* (Bruce and Schultz, 2001).

Common examples of this are when a person doesn't have the child, partner, job, or life they imagined or hoped to have. This might be because of illness or injury, infertility, trauma, divorce, or any number of other reasons.

4 CUMULATIVE GRIEF

Cumulative grief refers to the experience of suffering a new loss on top of an existing loss. It comes up when you suffer multiple losses in quick succession or at the same time. When you become overwhelmed by too much loss, your mind can activate an incredibly powerful defense mechanism—avoidance. This can leave you feeling like you can't address these multiple losses because it's all too overwhelming.

5 ABSENT (OR DELAYED) GRIEF

Absent grief is when you experience minimal emotional distress following a significant loss. It can be confusing, because you are expecting the intense emotions of grief only to find yourself numb. Absent grief is often thought to arise because of either shock, avoidance, or difficulty facing the painful emotional realities of the loss. There is no single cause for this type of grief experience, but you may be at greater risk if you were using substances at the time of the loss, have experienced multiple losses, have significant other stressors in your life, or if you were removed from the loss when it occurred, such as if you were on a military deployment, incarcerated, or living elsewhere (VandenBos, 2015).

6 PROLONGED GRIEF

In 2022, *prolonged grief disorder* (PGD), sometimes called *complicated grief,* was added to the *Diagnostic and Statistical Manual of Mental Disorders*

(DSM-5), a volume published by the American Psychiatric Association that defines and classifies mental disorders. This remains a controversial and divisive decision with far more nuance than we can capture in this list. But here's what we think you need to know as someone grieving:

Most people agree is that grief is a normal and natural response to loss and that it varies from person to person. Most also agree that some people struggle with intense grief for longer than others and experience greater difficulties coping with and tolerating grief. So where is the division? Some people believe that if a person is struggling with certain grief symptoms for an extended period, that is likely the result of PGD and they could benefit from professional intervention.

Others believe that struggling with certain grief symptoms for an extended period is likely the result of grief being an unpredictable and devastating event that impacts people in different ways for different durations and that is harder for some people to adapt to than others (for a whole host of reasons). Importantly, they do not believe this alone constitutes a mental disorder but agree that people who are struggling to adapt can benefit from professional support.

That may sound academic or clinical, but what we think is relevant to the average griever is actually pretty simple. First, you don't have to be labeled or meet criteria for a diagnosis to seek or receive help when grieving. Next, we have broader concerns about the societal impact of pathologizing grief. What our society deems "normal" or "healthy" in grief has changed significantly, even in the past thirty years, not to mention the cross-cultural variations. If we understand grief as the unique, ongoing, natural (albeit incredibly challenging) human response to a loss, the subjectivity and margin of error for mislabeling healthy grief as problematic are vast. Grief is complicated. If it weren't, you wouldn't have picked up this book.

Each of the types above has the potential to also be disenfranchised. Disenfranchised grief happens when you feel like society doesn't give you permission to grieve. It happens when you experience a loss that cannot be "openly acknowledged, socially sanctioned or publicly mourned" (Doka, 2002).

Just as society dictates unwritten rules for how to act, dress, speak, and operate in the world, society also dictates unwritten rules around grief. We get these messages from friends, family, community, and the media. They tell us what losses we have the right to grieve and when and how we're supposed to grieve them.

Ken Doka famously coined the phrase *disenfranchised grief* and explained that you're more likely to experience disenfranchised grief if:

- Society or your community doesn't recognize your loss as a loss
- Society or your community doesn't recognize you as someone grieving
- The loss was stigmatized in some way (like a death by suicide)
- The relationship was stigmatized (like an extramarital affair)
- The way that you are grieving doesn't match society's expectations of what grief looks like

---

OTHER LISTS TO CHECK OUT:

3 Questions About Feeling Nothing, page 99

8 Risk Factors for Experiencing Isolation, page 135

Make Your Own List: What's Your Grief? (Your List of Losses), page 39

8

Grief Theories That Are Not the Five Stages

While working with terminally ill patients in the 1960s, the Swiss American psychiatrist Elisabeth Kübler-Ross observed five stages people move between while they are dying: denial, anger, bargaining, depression, acceptance. These stages were later applied to people who were grieving. Though the stages were never intended to be experienced linearly or to comprehensively encompass grief, that's how they are often remembered.

Though Kübler-Ross's theory is the one you have likely heard about, there was much that came before her work and even more that's come since. Many of these writers and researchers have written volumes and we've distilled their work down to the main takeaway.

This is intended to give you the broadest of overviews, in case you'd like to do more research on your own. Most importantly, we hope it helps you to see how society absorbed some ideas from the early grief theories as to how people should grieve. Though grief theory has evolved significantly in the past one hundred years, the cultural conversation hasn't kept up with these changes.

what's your grief?

(1)

Sigmund Freud's Theory of Mourning
(1920s)

Freud was the first to suggest a theory as to how people should cope with grief. He said that to recover from grief, a person must express their grief and detach emotionally from the deceased.

(2)

Erich Lindemann's Grief Work Theory
(1940s)

Building on Freud's model, but coupling it with his own research observing individuals grieving after an unexpected loss, Lindemann theorized that one must complete the following tasks (*grief work*) to recover from grief:

- Emancipate from one's bondage to the deceased
- Readjust to a new environment where the deceased is missing
- Form new relationships

(3)

John Bowlby and Colin Murray Parkes's Four Stages of Grief
(1970s)

Bowlby and Parkes developed a theory of four stages of grief that a person must progress through in order to adapt to life after loss.

- Shock and numbness
- Yearning and searching
- Despair and disorganization
- Reorganization and recovery

4

J. William Worden's
Four Tasks of Mourning
(1980s)

Worden proposed that there are four tasks a person must complete in the process of mourning.

- Accept the reality of the loss
- Work through the pain of grief
- Adjust to an environment in which the deceased is missing
- Find an enduring connection with the deceased while embarking on a new life

Therese Rando's Six *R*s of Bereavement
(1980s)

Rando describes fluid processes that one must accomplish while grieving, broken down into what she calls the six *R*s of bereavement.

- Recognize the loss
- React to the separation
- Recollect and reexperience the deceased
- Relinquish old attachment
- Readjust to a new world
- Reinvest emotion energy

Simon Rubin's Two Tracks of Bereavement
(1990s)

This theory suggests that bereavement is a process experienced along two interactive axes or "tracks": an individual's biopsychosocial functioning (things like physical concerns, anxiety or depression, relationships, self-esteem, etc.), and their relationship with the deceased (things like emotional closeness to that person, conflict, positive and negative associations when thinking of the person, or preoccupation with the death). This theory suggests that to assess and cope with grief, someone needs to attend to both tracks of bereavement.

Stroebe and Schut's Dual Process Model of Grief
(1990s)

The dual process model suggests that grief is not about discrete stages or phases and is, instead, an ongoing process in which people oscillate between loss-related stressors and restoration-related stressors. The loss stressors are the things we more traditionally associate with grieving. The restoration stressors are related to everyday life, which doesn't stop for grief. Stroebe and Schut explain that it is important to tend to both of these domains and highlight that spending all of one's time trying to deal just with the loss stressors would be exhausting and neglect many of the other parts of living.

Klass, Silverman, and Nickman's
Continuing Bonds Theory
(1990s)

This theory upended the idea that grief was about "letting go" or "moving on" and says instead that people normally and naturally create continued connections with their loved ones who have died. These bonds are ongoing. They evolve over time and can be a normal, adaptive part of grieving.

OTHER LISTS TO CHECK OUT:

4 Places to Look for Grief Support in Your Community, page 256

3 FAQs About Coping with Life After Loss, page 172

4 Reasons to Love the Concept of Continuing Bonds, page 259

---

what's your grief?

What's Your Grief? (Your List of Losses)

The loss of something meaningful isn't just one earth-shattering loss. It is an immense loss, followed by a series of smaller losses in its aftermath. This domino effect of subsequent losses is known as *secondary loss*.

When you consider the impact of death, divorce, trauma, illness, and other significant losses, the inevitability of accompanying losses seems obvious. Yet, grieving people are often caught off guard by these ongoing losses and how they compound grief.

Secondary losses are also seldom formally acknowledged by supportive friends, family, and community members. We've yet to see a sympathy card that reads, "I am so sorry to hear you've lost faith in your fundamental belief system." Or, "My most heartfelt sympathies regarding the loss of half of your household income." Sure, those cards sound awkward and inappropriate, but therein lies the problem. Secondary losses are often so personal and private that it's difficult to give and receive support for them.

Though we can't list your secondary losses for you, knowing these four categories can help you begin to create your personal inventory.

Concrete Secondary Losses

Examples: losing a home, business, important objects, or finances

Relational Secondary Losses

Examples: losing friends who weren't supportive, losing family due to conflict, losing community as a result of a move

Belief System Secondary Losses

Examples: loss of hopes and dreams for the future, loss of a belief in a higher power, loss of faith in a fair, just, or safe world

Identity Secondary Losses

Examples: loss of role as a spouse or caregiver, loss of self-confidence, loss of career identity upon retirement, loss of physical or cognitive ability, independence, or autonomy

So here's what we want you to do:

We recommend you take time to assess your own secondary losses. Sometimes, seeing all these losses written down can provide a visual for just how complex the experience of grief actually is. In a practical sense, this exercise also helps you conceptualize what you need help coping with.

- Grab a sheet of paper or your journal.

- Write down your primary loss (or losses).

- Next, write down the secondary losses that were associated with the primary loss(es).

- If there are losses associated with these secondary losses, write those down too.

- As you're writing, notice if you hesitate to include secondary losses that seem less significant or disruptive. Push back on that impulse. This exercise is to help you reflect on the full impact of *your* grief, so you must include all your secondary losses—big and small.

what's your grief?

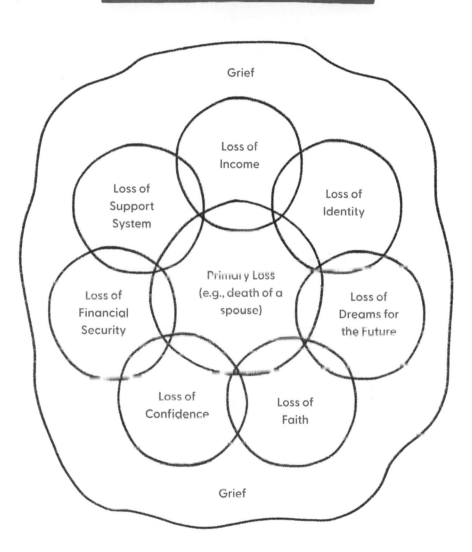

Grief

Loss of Income

Loss of Support System

Loss of Identity

Primary Loss (e.g., death of a spouse)

Loss of Financial Security

Loss of Dreams for the Future

Loss of Confidence

Loss of Faith

Grief

4

Ways New Losses Bring Up Old Ones

Cumulative loss is when a person experiences an accumulation of grief from multiple losses. We briefly introduced this concept when we discussed 7 Types of Grief You Should Know (but Probably Don't) on page 28. If you read up on cumulative loss, you'll notice it's typically used to describe two main scenarios.

The first scenario is when a person experiences losses that happen at the same time or one right after another. An example of this would be two loved ones dying a month apart. In this instance, the griever hardly has time to catch their breath before experiencing the second loss. Though each loss needs to be grieved in its own right, thoughts and feelings related to the overlapping losses get tangled together like two mixed-up balls of yarn.

The second scenario is when a person experiences a new loss before they've fully grieved a previous one. This scenario is far more general and, in our opinion, describes all losses. It's common to feel like a loss is never fully grieved. And experiencing new losses and going through times of hardship often stirs up painful thoughts and feelings related to past losses for many reasons, including the following.

1   LOSS MAKES YOU THINK ABOUT THE PAST.

Have you ever gone back to a place where you haven't been in a while and found yourself flooded with memories you hadn't thought of in years? That's because you were surrounded by context cues that improved your recall of memories tied to that place. Memory is funny like that; it isn't all neatly filed away. You can't reach in and access any memory at any time. Sometimes, memories only resurface when they're coaxed out with cues and triggers.

State-dependent memory is another type of memory cue. This cue triggers memories that are linked to specific physical or mental states. So when going through something stressful, it's normal to recall other distressing experiences from the past. For example, someone feeling angry at their spouse for forgetting to pick up the dry cleaning might suddenly be flooded with memories of other times they were mad at their spouse for entirely unrelated reasons. Or, when experiencing a new loss, a person may find that their emotional and physical responses strongly remind them of past loss experiences.

2   LOSS CAN MAKE YOU COMPARE YOUR CURRENT LOSS TO PAST LOSSES.

We'll caution you time and again about comparing your loss and grief to those of other people. However, when it comes to your own losses, it's normal and natural to think about how they compare. These comparisons may be helpful, and you might, for example, decide to use a particular coping skill because it was effective when grieving past losses. Or they may be frustrating, for example, if you feel that family and friends supported you more through a past loss.

3 LOSS CAN MAKE YOU THINK ABOUT WHAT MIGHT HAVE BEEN.

Another common way of thinking about loss is to contemplate alternative realities. This is called *counterfactual thinking*, and it's something we'll get into more in-depth later (see page 120). For now, it suffices to say that we sometimes see our losses as being causally connected, even when they aren't. For example, you might think, "If I hadn't been so distracted by my divorce, I would have been able to focus at work and wouldn't have lost out on that promotion." Or "If my mother hadn't died, she'd know how to help my sibling with her addiction and everything would be okay now."

4 NEW LOSSES CAN REMIND YOU THAT YOU'RE CAPABLE OF COPING WITH GRIEF.

When you're facing loss, it is sometimes helpful to think back and ask yourself, "How have I coped with hardship in the past?" In doing so, you may be able to identify helpful ways to cope. You might also notice the type of support you found valuable and comforting. Finally, you may find hope and strength in the knowledge that you were able to survive past losses and realize you will survive this one as well.

OTHER LISTS TO CHECK OUT:

7 Types of Grief You Should Know (but Probably Don't), page 28

4 Things That Can Happen When You Compare Losses, page 139

4 Facts to Remember When Life Doesn't Turn Out
the Way You Planned, page 270

4

Obstacles to Grieving
Nondeath Losses

On page 39, we asked you to list the losses that brought you to this book. If it's been a while since you wrote the list, take a minute to review it. If you didn't write a list, that's okay! Simply think for a few minutes about the significant loss (or losses) you're currently grappling with.

Whether or not you're grieving a death loss, we're willing to bet you've felt the impact of a nondeath loss at some point, especially when you consider that secondary losses are usually nondeath losses. As with all types of loss, nondeath losses come with their own set of challenges.

①
Nondeath losses are less likely
to be recognized by society.

Our society seems pretty comfortable with the following logic: "If there has been a death, then there will be grief." From an early age, the correlation between death and grief is so ingrained in us that many begin to believe the reverse logic is true: "If there is no death, there is no grief." You know this statement is false because, as we've discussed, you can grieve the loss of *anything* significant to you. Unfortunately, though, this is a truth most people must arrive at through personal experience. And because many people don't make accommodations for the grief of divorce, infertility, disability, and so on, people grieving nondeath losses seldom receive meaningful acknowledgment or support from others.

(2)
Nondeath losses are often personal and private.

Loss of self-worth, questioning one's faith, or miscarriage in early pregnancy are losses that are often shared with just a few people, if anyone at all. Though some people may openly acknowledge these losses, many won't, making it difficult for people to give (and receive) support for them.

(3)
Nondeath losses aren't always easy for *you* to identify.

People don't often see a nondeath loss for what it is. Instead, they categorize it alongside other difficult life experiences like obstacles, setbacks, and bumps in the road. Though most loss experiences are also these things, such categorizations don't acknowledge the element of the experience that needs to be grieved.

(4)
People are often caught off guard by how difficult nondeath losses are.

Humans aren't great at accurately predicting how they will feel in the future. Though someone might be able to say, for example, that they'd feel terrible if they lost their job, they don't know exactly how horrible they'd feel and for how long. At the same time, they might not anticipate other thoughts and emotions like anger over their unjust firing, relief at not being required to work a job that wasn't a good fit, or suddenly feeling unworthy or undeserving. Unlike with death loss, which people usually realize is going to be life-altering, people often underestimate the impact of nondeath loss.

OTHER LISTS TO CHECK OUT:

5 Little-Known Truths About Grief, page 19

Make Your Own List: What's Your Grief? (Your List of Losses), page 39

5 Items for Your Grief Not-to-Do List, page 58

6

Life Domains
Impacted by Loss

Grief isn't just about feelings. The reality is that grief is a constellation of thoughts, feelings, and experiences that impacts the emotional, cognitive, behavioral, spiritual, physical, and existential domains of life. Reflecting on each domain can allow you to see where grief may be impacting that area.

1 YOUR FEELINGS

Grief can send your emotions into overdrive, leaving you with more feelings than you have ever felt and feeling them more intensely than ever before. Emotions can cycle quickly or last for months. Emotions that feel like they're contradictory can occur at the exact same time. Calling it an emotional roller coaster is an understatement.

2 YOUR THOUGHTS

Grief isn't just about how you feel; it's about how you think. There's a good chance you've found your brain overflowing with thoughts—painful thoughts, complicated thoughts, overwhelming thoughts. "I'll never be happy again." "I made a huge mistake." "It's all his fault." "No one understands." The list of loss-related thoughts goes on and on and on. Understanding these is a huge part of learning to cope with grief, so we'll spend a good bit of time on thoughts in Part Two.

3 YOUR BEHAVIOR

After your life was shattered by loss, you may have found yourself doing things you'd never done, behaving in ways you'd never behaved. You may find yourself snapping at people when you used to stay cool. You might isolate yourself when you're usually a social butterfly. Maybe you never liked to shop and suddenly find yourself on a first-name basis with the Amazon delivery driver. Long and short, grief changes your behaviors.

4 YOUR BELIEFS

Be it religion or simply your connection to things beyond yourself, losses big and small can impact your spiritual belief system. Whether your faith was shaken or you're questioning your faith in good things coming back around to good people, grief can destabilize your spiritual world. On the other end of the spectrum, for some people grief strengthens spirituality, helping them find greater comfort in religion or a higher power. A new-found awakening to the universality of human suffering leaves some people feeling a deeper spiritual connection with humanity.

5 YOUR HEALTH

One question that hits our inbox almost every week is, "I'm having [*insert physical symptom here*]. Could it be grief?" The short answer: ask your doctor; better safe than sorry. The long answer: loss can trigger all sorts of physiological responses, including sleeping too much, not sleeping enough, forgetfulness, attention difficulties, eating too much, not eating enough, headaches, stomach pains, muscle aches, and more.

6 YOUR PURPOSE

The Danish philosopher Søren Kierkegaard suggested that existential crisis can arise when your worldview isn't able to accommodate unexpected life circumstances, which often occurs after loss or trauma. Anything that brings into awareness the passage of time, suffering, and the impermanence of life can leave you questioning your purpose.

You may find your brain flooded with questions like "Does any of this matter?" and "Aren't we all just going to die and be forgotten?" Though such questions can bring up deep feelings of angst and dread, these existential experiences are a normal part of human development and maturation (Yalom, 1980).

OTHER LISTS TO CHECK OUT:

6 Mixed-Up Emotions You May Feel in Loss, page 70

4 Mind Tricks That Complicate Grief, page 120

6 Ways Grief Can Change Your Priorities, page 145

5

Ws to Help You Understand Support Systems

At some point in your childhood, an adult probably handed you crayons and a blank sheet of paper and asked you to draw a picture of your family. You might have eagerly colored a stick-figure drawing of yourself holding hands with a much larger stick-figure person—a parent or grandparent, perhaps. Maybe there were other grown-ups there as well, along with siblings, pets, imaginary friends, and all the other important people in your world.

Now, imagine we asked you to draw a similar picture of the people who care for you today. What would it look like? Would there be parents, siblings, friends, your therapist? Would someone important be missing? Would you struggle to draw the picture because you're no longer sure whom to include?

Your support system can significantly impact your grief in both positive and negative ways. For this reason, we're asking you to start thinking about your support safety net now while we're focusing on the basics. We'll talk more about assessing your support system on page 230. But in the meantime, we want you to compose a general picture of your support system in your mind. Specifically, the who, what, where, when, and why.

1 · Who?

A support system is a group of people who work together, both directly and indirectly, to provide help and assistance to a member of the system. This makes the work of a support system sound very active, and sometimes, especially during times of crisis, it is. But when life is calm, the support system is more like a reserve of people who can step up and help when needed.

We are all at the center of our own support systems, but we're also a part of other people's support systems. This means that it's our job to take care of ourselves as well as others. In a perfect world, we'd each take turns needing support, but sometimes a loss impacts an entire group of people, and that's when things can get tricky. We think it's helpful to think of your support system as being made up of different tiers. Your close family and friends are on the first tiers. More distant people, like community members and professionals, would be on a further tier. When your first tier of support is also dealing with loss, everyone may struggle to get their needs met. In these instances, it may be helpful to look to your second or third tier for help.

2 · What?

Support can range from helping someone meet practical needs to offering emotional support to providing comic relief. Ideally, your support system can meet a wide range of needs, but sometimes it's enough to know that you have people in your corner when you need them. Over the years, one of the most consistent things we've heard grievers say they need from their support systems is to be shown, through words and actions, that their support system will be there for them now and in the future.

3 · Where?

Anywhere! Support can be informal, like catching up over a cup of coffee, or it can take place in a structured setting, like seeing a therapist or support group. Support can happen via a check-in text, online (through virtual support forums, for example), or over the good old-fashioned house phone.

4 · When?

Good grief support is ongoing. It doesn't end after the casseroles stop rolling in. Ideally, there will be people in your life who continue to check in and whom you can reach out to on bad days, even years after your loss.

5 · Why?

To paraphrase the Beatles, you get by with a little help from your friends. No, this isn't just a catchy line; research shows that there are many positive physical health and mental health benefits to having good social support during times of loss, trauma, and hardship (Hibberd et al., 2010).

We don't want to leave you with the sense that you're doomed if you don't have a stellar support system behind you. If we're honest, most people feel their support system is lacking in some way. In these instances, we recommend looking in your community for groups, organizations, and professionals who can help fill gaps in your existing support network.

OTHER LISTS TO CHECK OUT:

Make Your Own List: What Are Your Grief Support Needs?, page 228

3 To-Dos for Utilizing Your Support System, page 230

4 Places to Look for Grief Support in Your Community, page 256

What's Your Grief Style?

Though we remain grateful that Elisabeth Kübler-Ross's Five Stages of Grief opened up a new conversation about dying and grief in our culture, they brought with them a prevalent and problematic misconception—that grief looks generally the same for most people. By now it should be clear that your grief is unique to you—no stages, no timeline.

That said, we've noticed some common styles in how people grieve. They are not universal and they exist on a spectrum. They overlap with one another, and you likely have different tendencies at different times. Keep in mind, none of these styles is better or worse than another. They are just different ways people cope with loss.

The Intuitive Griever

Kenneth Doka and Terry Martin coined the terms *intuitive grief* and *instrumental grief*. Through their research into styles of grief, they found that most people fell into these two types. Intuitive grief is when a person has a strong emotional experience and the outward expression of their grief mirrors those inner feelings. This is the style often thought of as "normal" grief in white European American culture. If this is your grief style, you might find yourself wanting to express your emotions through talking or writing, or even yelling and screaming.

The Instrumental Griever

The other grief style that Doka and Martin observed was less accepted in many Western cultures. Instrumental grievers often have a more cognitive experience of grief, processing the loss through their thoughts. These grievers are less likely to show emotions outwardly, and instead they often describe the physical pain of grief. They tend to keep thinking about the person or events that led to the loss. What helps them is often action oriented, like dealing with estate issues or planning a memorial fund. The tricky thing about this style is that some people will think you aren't grieving because you aren't showing your emotions. You are—your grief just isn't the intuitive style many think of.

The Introverted Griever

Whether you are introverted or extroverted impacts your default ways of experiencing many things in life, and grief is no exception. If you're an introvert coping with loss, you can still benefit from strong social support and time with others. But even the most supportive social interactions can leave you needing alone time to recharge. It's important, however, that the comfort of alone time doesn't slip into social isolation. You may find yourself less interested in support groups as a way to cope with grief and that is A-OK, as long as you are seeking other coping outlets that work for you.

The Extroverted Griever

After a loss, some extroverts find themselves turning inward in ways they aren't used to—declining social invitations and even phone calls because it just feels like too much. Other extroverts may throw themselves into being with other people, either to find a space to express their thoughts and feelings or as a way to avoid being alone with their thoughts and feelings. If you're an extrovert, it's crucial to find some key support people, while also taking time to be alone with your grief so that social interaction doesn't turn into avoidance.

The Optimistic Griever

Optimistic people and pessimistic people tell themselves different stories about why things happen to them and the duration and degree of the impact of those things. The way you explain difficult life events is connected to your worldview, and that explanation can deeply impact your grief. In his 2006 book *Learned Optimism*, the world-renowned psychologist Martin Seligman describes this by saying that when bad things happen to an optimist, the optimist is more likely to think that things happen by chance and circumstance, that difficult circumstances will pass relatively quickly, and that life will be impacted but it will go on. Because optimistic grievers tend to believe the negative impact of difficult life events will not be permanent, it is easier for them to remain hopeful even in dire situations. Let's be clear about one thing, though. This doesn't make their grief any less painful. It just means that finding hope after loss might come more naturally to you as an optimist.

The Pessimistic Griever

Pessimists are more likely to tell a cynical story after something difficult has happened. Seligman's research finds that pessimists are more likely to blame themselves (whether they had any culpability or not) for bad things that happen, to believe the impact will last forever, and to feel everything else they do will be detrimentally affected by the negative event. Seligman also found that people who lean pessimistic tend to think of bad things as more permanent. If someone at work snaps at a pessimist, they are more likely to think, "she's a nasty person," rather than, "she must be having a bad day" (Seligman, 2006). After a loss, a person with pessimistic leanings can find it more difficult to be hopeful, because their default is to assume that the negative impact of grief will be permanent. If you're a pessimist, don't panic! This doesn't mean you're fated to never find hope after loss. It just means you'll need to do some more deliberate and focused coping.

what's your grief?

So here's what we want you to do:

- We have a feeling from reading the descriptions above that you might have a sense of your leanings. They are each on a spectrum and most people fall somewhere in between the extremes.

- Take a moment now to consider your tendencies and where you think you fall on these spectrums. This will prove helpful not only in increasing your self-awareness but also as you consider the grief support tools that might be most useful to you.

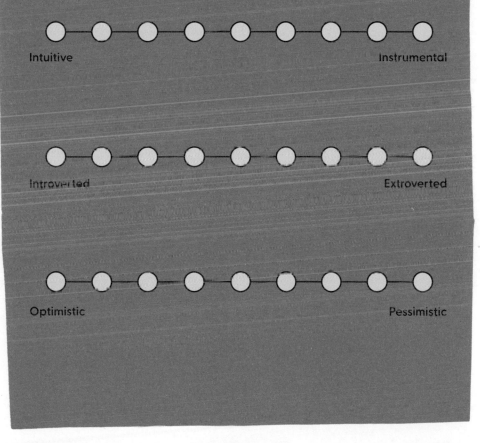

Intuitive   Instrumental

Introverted   Extroverted

Optimistic   Pessimistic

5

Items for Your Grief
Not-to-Do List

We're big fans of to-do lists. Not only do they help you stay organized, but planning eases anxiety, and checking boxes helps provide a sense of accomplishment.

Not-to-do lists serve a different purpose. They remind you of the things that prevent you from living life the way you'd like, whatever that means for you. This particular list focuses on not doing things that get in the way of coping with grief and that complicate life after loss.

(1)
Don't talk yourself
out of your grief.

Sometimes people tell themselves their loss isn't worthy of grief, they aren't deserving of support, or they've been grieving too long. But it doesn't matter what type of loss you experienced or how long ago you experienced it; your feelings are real and valid. Whether you're comfortable openly acknowledging your loss is up to you, but know that outright denying it isn't going to make it go away.

(2)

Don't bully yourself.

There is no right or wrong way to grieve a loss. Thoughts and emotions aren't inherently right, wrong, good, or bad. It is only through your perception of these internal experiences that you might label them one way or another.

Of course, thoughts and emotions often result in *behaviors*, and if you feel guilty about something you've said or done in a low moment, well, we've all been there. Give yourself a little grace; no one is at their best when they're grieving.

(3)

Don't lock your grief monster in a closet.

In the beginning, grief seems entirely too overwhelming and frightening. Scared and unsure how to cope, many people try to shut their grief away in a dark place. Their grief is like a monster they want to run from for fear it will gobble them up if they turn to face it.

But here's the thing about monsters hiding in closets, ducked under beds, or lurking in dark corners: usually when you flip on a light and get a good look, you realize they aren't as scary as you believed them to be. Most of the fear and anxiety lies in anticipating the unknown. When you look at grief with the intention of getting to know it, you'll often find that it looks very different than you expected.

(4)

Don't write off
all of humankind.

If one more person minimizes your feelings or mocks you with an inspirational Instagram meme, you're going to lose it—we get it. People often don't know how to help grieving family members and friends, so their attempts can be awkward and insensitive, at a time when your poor nerves are already worn thin.

All that said, please don't give up on people. Grieving people often share that loss helped them forge even deeper relationships with those who "get it" and that they made new connections in their grief (we call these people *grief friends* and when you find them, you'll never want to lose them).

(5)

Don't think the darkness
will never end.

We are easily convinced of the abiding truth of our current circumstances. Our bodies are ever-aging, our emotions are constantly in flux, and our external world is always changing. Yet, there is nothing we believe in quite so earnestly as the reality of our present moment.

After something really, truly terrible happens, the darkness has a way of coming on fast. You feel twisted and turned by intense emotion, and you free-fall into a place with no obvious path out. You can't envision ever feeling anything other than pain, and in these moments your circumstances seem eternal.

But rest assured, the impact of grief changes over time. The fog will start to thin as you learn to understand grief differently and find new ways to cope with it, and you'll begin to see the path forward with greater clarity. Though grief comes in waves, remember that happiness also comes in waves. Even though the future that lies ahead may look different than you ever imagined, there will be space for hope, healing, purpose, and meaning.

OTHER LISTS TO CHECK OUT:

3 Things to Know About Avoidance, page 78

5 Ways to Get Comfortable with Grief, page 206

Make Your Own List: What's Your Hope?, page 286

PART TWO

The Wide Range of Grief

We spent the first section of this book trying to help you understand more about grief—what it is, what it isn't, when it happens, and some things we think you should know about it. We also told you that there is a lot we can't tell you. There are too many variables for grief to be universal or predictable.

You might be asking, where do those variables come from? Fair question. The simple answer is they come from *you*. We each come to loss with a unique history that led us to that moment. We are all surrounded by our unique circle of family and friends. We have distinctive personalities and coping styles. We've had to weather different storms. We have different ways of processing feelings. We all have particular modes of thinking and communicating. We each have our own relationship with who or what we've lost.

These amazing quirks are what make each of us who we are. They're also what make the trajectory of grief so tricky to predict. Your grief is the emotional, cognitive, behavioral, spiritual, physical, existential experience that you will live after your loss. It won't be the same for anyone else because no one else feels, thinks, acts, wonders, worries, copes, or creates exactly the way you do.

This means we can't create a checklist that works for all people to understand and cope with loss—that's the bad news. But there is good news too. The more you understand about yourself, the more you can get to know your grief. It will never be predictable, but it can slowly start to feel a bit more manageable.

In Part One we taught you some of the things we know about grief and loss. In Part Two, we're going to walk you through some of the most common reactions to loss. This will help you dig into your grief self-exploration, which can feel intimidating without some direction. Some reactions will apply to you, some won't. Some will apply to you even though you think they don't.

Before we dive in, we want to share a little concept in psychology put forth by the psychiatrist Aaron Beck in the 1960s. He proposed that the way we humans experience situations or events is deeply impacted by our reactions to those situations or events. He introduced the idea that when something happens to us, it triggers thoughts. We then have feelings about those thoughts, and those feelings drive our behaviors, which then lead to more thoughts and more feelings and more behaviors, on and on.

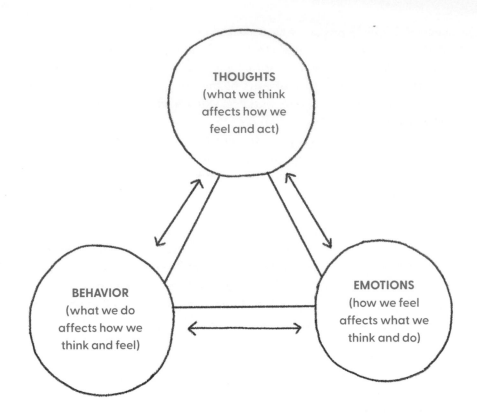

Let's look at a quick example. Imagine you and a colleague are both laid off from your jobs due to budget cuts.

Your colleague thinks to himself, "I can't believe they laid me off. That was my dream job. I always screw things up. I'll never find such a good job again." These thoughts cause a sea of feeling to swell up in him. He feels insecurity, shame, embarrassment, anxiety, and hopelessness. Those emotions then drive his behaviors: He tells very few people what has happened because he's ashamed. He procrastinates looking for a new job for weeks, thinking he'll never find another good job again and feeling hopeless. When he finally starts looking, he doesn't apply for the best jobs, assuming future employers will view the layoff as his fault.

Meanwhile, let's imagine that you think to yourself, "Wow, this layoff is really disappointing. I loved that job and I have a lot of bills to pay. But it wasn't my fault, the budget was out of my control. I was able to land that job, so if I start looking now I'll be able to find another good job." Though the circumstances were the same, your thoughts are very different from your colleague's. Your emotions then look different as well. You feel disappointed and worried, but optimistic. Your behaviors also take a divergent path from those of your colleague. Without the same feelings of self-blame, you tell your friends and family about the loss, who are supportive and reassuring. This helps your self-confidence and you begin applying for jobs right away.

The different experiences people can have after experiencing the same loss illustrate how the relationship between your thoughts, emotions, and behaviors can deeply impact how you experience and respond to the surprises life throws at you. The way you process a loss isn't better or worse than the way someone else does. No one's thoughts or feelings are right or wrong. They're different, and in these differences lies the nuance of your grief.

The lists in this section explore the common things that people *think*, *feel*, and *do* after a significant loss. A section on this topic could never cover everything that has or will come up in your grief. But we have included those that research and personal and professional experience all tell us are commonly encountered.

When a loss shatters your world, the grief is often nothing like you'd imagined. You may be thinking, feeling, and doing things that you've never thought, felt, or done. If you've found yourself overwhelmed by, confused by, and even scared of your own grief reactions, you're not alone. One of the most common question we're asked is, "Is this normal?"

This section's lists are meant to answer that question. And we hope they will give you the space to better identify, explore, and understand your unique grief responses.

What Are Your Grief Emotions?

Though grief is so much more than an emotional experience, the overwhelming feelings that come up are often the first things people worry and wonder about. You will experience feelings that arise for the first time; feelings that change from hour to hour or minute to minute. One emotion bleeds into another. It is not uncommon to be overwhelmed with emotion while struggling to identify what some of the emotions even are.

As we start talking more about feelings, it makes sense to begin with a comprehensive list of the most common feelings that come up in the wake of loss. This list is not exhaustive, of course. You may recognize feelings in yourself that aren't on this list. That's good. The important work is to reflect on which of these feelings are part of your grief (and make notes of those we left off but that feel significant for you).

So here's what we want you to do:

- Using the list on page 69, write down on a piece of paper the emotions that have most impacted you since your loss. Feel free to also add any not listed.

- Once you've done that, circle the two emotions that you find yourself struggling with most often.

- In the spirit of recognizing the relationship between thoughts and feelings, make note of any thoughts that you associate with those emotions.

- Hard as it may be, try not to judge these emotions and thoughts. Just observe them.

Abandoned	Exhausted	Nostalgic
Afraid	Frustrated	Nothing
Alienated	Grateful	Numb
Alive	Grounded	Overloaded
Alone	Guilty	Overwhelmed
Angry	Gutted	Panicked
Anguished	Heartbroken	Paralyzed
Anxious	Heavy	Powerless
Ashamed	Helpless	Reconnected
Bereft	Hollow	Regretful
Betrayed	Hopeful	Relieved
Brave	Hopeless	Resentful
Broken	Human	Sad
Compassionate	Impatient	Scared
Conflicted	Inadequate	Shattered
Confused	Incomplete	Shocked
Connected	Indifferent	Sick
Crazy	In pain	Silenced
Dead inside	Insane	Small
Defeated	Insecure	Split apart
Depersonalized	Invincible	Strong
Depleted	Invisible	Stunned
Depressed	Isolated	Tired
Despairing	Jealous	Trapped
Desperate	Joyless	Unmotivated
Devastated	Liberated	Unseen
Different	Lonely	Unsettled
Directionless	Longing	Unworthy
Disbelieving	Lost	Vulnerable
Disconnected	Loving	Wanting
Disoriented	Mad	Weak
Drowning	Melancholy	Weary
Empathetic	Miserable	Withdrawn
Empty	Misunderstood	Yearning

6

Mixed-Up Emotions
You May Feel in Loss

Since you lived through whatever difficult life event brought you to this book, you've probably heard the question "How are you feeling?" more times than you'd care to count.

It sounds so simple, doesn't it? But the question of what you're feeling can be shockingly complicated.

Living with loss forces you to create space for your tangled thoughts, emotions, and desires to exist alongside one another. This requires the flexibility to feel two seemingly opposite things at the exact same time. This is not a checklist of all the emotional contradictions you'll stumble upon, but rather a few common examples that we see regularly.

You are looking forward to the future, but are sad to leave the past behind.

Example: You know in your heart that divorce is the right decision for you and your partner and feel optimistic about life on your own, but you also deeply miss the comfort and intimacy you once shared with your spouse and the life you thought you would have together. This excitement about the future life does not take away from the pain of grieving the life you thought you would share.

(2)
You are genuinely happy for someone else, but also jealous of them.

Example: Your dear friend gets pregnant while you and your partner are struggling with infertility. You are both truly and completely happy for your friend, while also feeling some jealousy that you have not been able to conceive. This jealousy does not detract from the joy you feel for your friend. It exists alongside it. That's entirely normal but feels . . . complicated.

(3)
You would give anything to change the past, but you also know that surviving it has made you a stronger person.

Example: When you reflect on the person you've become since your sister's death, you recognize that you have a deeper appreciation for life, more substantive relationships, and greater strength than you ever imagined. At the same time, you want your sister back and sometimes feel guilt for appreciating how you've changed. Your gratitude for the growth you've experienced in no way diminishes the degree to which you wish your sister had survived. You would trade the growth to have your sister back, but because that is not a possibility, you can still recognize and value the person you are as a result of the loss.

(4)

You are devastated about a loss, but at the same time feel a sense of relief.

Example: After caring for your mother with dementia for seven years in your home, her needs are beyond what you can provide and she must move to a memory facility. You feel devastated that she is continuing to decline and that you cannot provide the care that she needs. At the same time, you feel relief—followed by a pang of immense guilt for feeling relieved. You can simultaneously wish that your mother's condition had not deteriorated and that she was still able to live with you, while also acknowledging that caregiving is incredibly hard work and that it is normal to feel grateful for assistance and respite.

(5)

You love someone entirely while feeling profoundly angry with them.

Example: Your seventeen-year-old daughter has a substance use disorder and has begun stealing from you and disappearing for days on end. You love her as deeply and unconditionally as you ever have, while also feeling previously unimaginable anger, fear, and exasperation. You feel all of these emotions simultaneously and wholeheartedly.

(6)

You intensely miss someone you are grieving, but also love and care for someone new.

Example: After four years of widowhood, you finally feel ready to date. You meet someone new with whom you have a connection. This is deeply comforting and also makes you miss your partner even more. The feelings for this new person in no way diminish the love for your late partner, and vice versa. These feelings can coexist.

Grief opens your eyes to a world in which the sun and rain can exist in the same moment. This reality can be a bit disorienting at first but, in many ways, it is a good thing. It means that you don't have to choose between grieving the past and living in the present. It means that the pain of loss can exist right alongside things like gratitude, happiness, and hope.

OTHER LISTS TO CHECK OUT:

4 Things You Can Do to Cope with Conflicting Emotions, page 193

9 Ways to Be Kind to Yourself While Grieving, page 200

4 Tips for Finding Calm in Your Grief Storm, page 203

5

Realities of Acute Stress

Before, during, and after a big loss or major life transition, your once-comfortable world might feel like an unrecognizable sea of loss, confusion, chaos, and questions. You might have lived through an event that threatened your physical safety or that of someone else. You might have lived through something that destabilized you emotionally. In the face of fear and uncertainty, your body's biological responses kick into overdrive.

①

Your body's natural reaction to stress is the *acute stress response.*

When you perceive a circumstance as extremely threatening to your safety and well-being, your body is hard-wired to respond. Though evolutionarily we developed this trait so we could flee from predators, you don't need a lion chasing you for your acute stress response to kick into gear. It is triggered anytime you face a situation that your brain processes as a threat. Learning that you have a serious illness, that someone died, that a loved one was hurt, or that your partner is leaving you yanks your sense of emotional and physical safety out from under you. In a matter of seconds, your brain recognizes the danger, it sends out a distress call, and your sympathetic nervous system responds. Suddenly your body is firing off adrenaline (aka epinephrine), giving you energy to protect yourself.

(2)

The acute stress response is your
body's effort to protect you.

When you notice your heart pounding, your breath quickening, and your blood pressure spiking, it might not feel like your body is doing you any favors. What you're experiencing is the response of the sympathetic nervous system. This system is also known as the *fight-or-flight* system because it primes you to either stay and fight the threat, run for your life, or remain paralyzed and motionless (that last one might not sound all that adaptive, but from an evolutionary perspective it works; a predator might become disinterested or, if you couldn't escape, you'd at least be able to psychologically detach or numb to reduce your pain). Unfortunately, the brain doesn't always differentiate between types of threats.

(3)

Though the acute stress response is totally normal,
the symptoms feel anything but.

These can include physical symptoms such as increased heart rate, rapid breathing, muscle tension, feeling sick to your stomach, light headedness, chest pain, headache, and abdominal pain. It can also include psychological symptoms like feeling detached or numb, feelings of derealization (alienation, confusion, disconnection from those around you, and unfamiliarity with your surroundings), feelings of depersonalization (feeling like you are outside of yourself and observing yourself), loss of memory, intrusive thoughts, increased arousal, hypervigilance, problems concentrating, avoidance, or anxiety.

Your acute stress reaction should subside once the threat has passed.

There is a common analogy therapists often use to explain the acute stress response: Imagine your body is a car and adrenaline is the gas you need to respond in a crisis. The first part of the acute stress reaction is your brain putting the pedal to the metal, flooding that adrenaline into the engine so you can respond. The second part of the acute stress response is your brain figuring out what to do next. In an ideal world, after that first surge of gas, your brain keeps assessing the world around you to see if the danger has dissipated. If it has, it eases off the gas and your body starts to calm down. If it hasn't, it keeps the foot on the pedal. Most of the time your brain gets it right, but not always. Sometimes after significant trauma or loss, your brain keeps flooring it. This means your nervous system is still in overdrive, your stress hormones are still pumping, and you're having physical and psychological symptoms long after the event. If this keeps up for more than two days and up to thirty days, it is known as an *acute stress disorder*. If it keeps up for more than a month, it is known as *post-traumatic stress*. If you're concerned about this, talk to a therapist or psychiatrist who can assess your symptoms.

It's common to fear your own reactions.

We know, this sounds pretty meta. But bear with us. After experiencing a devastating event, a person often looks at how they handled, or are handling, the event. Depending on the intensity of your loss and the degree to which your brain perceived it as threatening, you may have felt, thought, said, or done countless things that you can't make sense of as you reflect on them. Maybe you lashed out at people. Perhaps you shut down completely, paralyzed by fear. Maybe you avoided the situation. If you can't

what's your grief?

make sense of what you did—whatever that was—it might feel frightening. You might worry this means you can't cope or handle crises. You might judge yourself for reactions that don't, on the surface, make sense. If any of this sounds familiar, take a few minutes to consider whether they might have been part of your body's normal physiological stress response.

OTHER LISTS TO CHECK OUT:

5 Ways to Get Comfortable with Grief, page 206

Make Your Own List: What's Your Grief Trigger?, page 210

4 Tips for Finding Calm in Your Grief Storm, page 203

3

Things to Know
About Avoidance

Imagine a time when you felt okay about life. Maybe you even felt good, in control, protected, calm, capable, or strong. When you left your house each morning, you had no reason to assume that danger would befall you, so you felt safe to wander the world.

Now, imagine you live in a world that seems filled with danger. When we speak of danger, we mean the kind that's genuinely threatening to your physical safety. But we also mean the things that can't hurt you physically but that you subjectively perceive as emotionally painful—things like reminders of your loss, threats to your sense of self, and uncomfortable interactions at the grocery store.

You may not have to imagine these emotional threats because they parallel your current reality. Perhaps since your loss, the world feels more threatening, people seem uncaring, and you feel less capable of handling the stress of it all. Suddenly, it feels hazardous to wander the world freely because the shattered and jagged fragments of your loss seem embedded in every corner of your life. For many people, this is where avoidance comes in.

1

Avoidance means avoiding your feelings, not people or situations.

When we talk about avoidance with regard to grief, we are usually referring to *experiential avoidance*. In a nutshell, experiential avoidance is focused on avoiding unpleasant feelings. It includes efforts to block out, reduce, or change distressing thoughts, emotions, or bodily sensations.

This is an important distinction to make because at face value, you might think that what's being avoided is a person, place, or thing. However, in experiential avoidance you are avoiding how that person, place, or thing makes you feel. For example, someone whose spouse recently died might avoid her friend's twenty-fifth anniversary party not because she's unsupportive of her friend or anti anniversary parties, but because the experience might trigger painful thoughts and emotions related to her own loss.

2

Temporary avoidance can be helpful.

Emphasis on *temporary*. As you know, grief doesn't happen in a bubble. Life goes on, and sometimes you need to tell your grief to go away for a bit so you can get things done. Also, sometimes you need a brief reprieve from the intensity of your grief, and this temporary avoidance can be healthy. And finally, sometimes you're just not ready to face certain things, so you avoid them until you feel stronger.

(3) Prolonged avoidance can be harmful.

For many, avoidance can become a harmful cycle that persists to the detriment of healing. Many people mistakenly think that if they avoid their feelings for long enough, painful emotions will fade away with time. But in reality, time does *not* heal all wounds, and deliberate attempts to suppress specific thoughts often make them more likely to surface. (To illustrate, whatever you do, do *not* think of a white bear. What did you think of?)

Not only does avoidance intensify anxious thoughts, it also prevents you from dealing with them. By avoiding the scenarios you fear, you never learn that (a) most of the time they can't hurt you, (b) sometimes they aren't as awful as anticipated, and (c) even when they are, you are capable of tolerating them.

Finally, and perhaps most importantly, avoiding grief-related thoughts and emotions cuts you off from people, places, and things that at one time were important to you. As you avoid more, your world gets smaller and smaller, and you become less able to find new sources of connection, comfort, and purpose.

OTHER LISTS TO CHECK OUT:

5 Signs You Are Practicing Avoidance, page 81

5 Reactions You May Have to a Chaotic and Uncontrollable World, page 88

5 Ways to Get Comfortable with Grief, page 206

5

Signs You Are
Practicing Avoidance

Once you have a basic understanding of avoidance, the next step is identifying the role it plays in your life.

Avoidance can be difficult to spot because it underlies behaviors, and not all these behaviors are inherently problematic. It can sometimes take a bit of time and introspection to spot harmful avoidance. So to get you started, here are a few general ways avoidance might show up in your day-to-day life.

1 YOU ARE WITHDRAWING FROM PEOPLE, PLACES, AND ACTIVITIES.

When the world feels unsafe, it seems logical to stay home. And that's what many people do after a loss. They avoid anyone, anywhere, and anything that might trigger painful grief-related emotions.

2 YOU ARE TELLING YOURSELF AND OTHERS YOU ARE FINE.

If "I'm fine" has become your default response to everyone, even yourself, it might be a sign of avoidance. Perhaps you don't want to admit you're struggling because it makes you feel weak or vulnerable. Maybe it's been a while since your loss, and you think people will judge you for continuing to grieve. Or perhaps you're worried if you tell a friend or family member that you're having a difficult time, they'll try to help you, and you don't want to feel pressured to take their advice.

3 YOU ARE PROCRASTINATING.

It's logical that one might use procrastination to avoid grief's more uncomfortable feelings. A person might avoid dating long after a breakup because they fear being rejected again. Or someone may put off sorting through a deceased loved one's belongings because they know it will be emotional. We always advocate for waiting until you feel ready to take on challenging tasks, if you can. But it's also important to recognize if you're putting off an activity for longer than is reasonable or feasible. For example, you may be holding off on selling your late brother's car because parting with it will be incredibly emotional. But if you don't have space to keep it, it may not be reasonable to delay.

4 YOU ARE DISTRACTING YOURSELF.

A person may seek distraction after loss to avoid facing painful thoughts, memories, and emotions. Distraction can take many forms, including throwing yourself into activities, staying as busy as possible, working long hours, or focusing all your mental energy on supporting other people.

5   YOU ARE USING SUBSTANCES.

Using mind-altering substances is a common form of avoidance. When you aren't sober, you either don't feel the pain as intensely or don't really care. This is dangerous because you'll need to take more and more of the substance to numb the pain of grief, and you never learn constructive ways to cope with distressing thoughts and emotions.

OTHER LISTS TO CHECK OUT:

3 Things to Know About Avoidance, page 78

5 Facts About Rumination, page 94

8 Risk Factors for Experiencing Isolation, page 135

6

Causes of Grief-Related Anxiety

One doesn't either have anxiety or not have anxiety. Everyone experiences it to some extent. What varies are the thoughts, feelings, and experiences that cause individual anxiety, the intensity of the anxiety, and how different people respond to and cope with it.

You may experience little to no anxiety at certain times in your life, for example, when you're engaged in an activity that relaxes you. Other times, you may experience a moderate amount of anxiety, such as when taking a test or giving a presentation at work (unless you have a fear of tests or public speaking). Anxiety that falls in the middle of the continuum is usually healthy because it helps keep you on track, motivates you, and keeps you reasonably vigilant against threats to your health or physical safety.

But there are times when you may experience anxiety that falls on the high end of the spectrum. If you have ever experienced an anxiety disorder like a phobia or generalized anxiety disorder, you know that these conditions tend to involve heightened and frequent anxiety. Other instances of high anxiety may occur at specific times in your life. For example, experiencing a loss or trauma can change and intensify your experience with anxiety for many reasons, a few of which we'll discuss here.

(1)

You are trying to avoid unpleasant thoughts, memories, and emotions.

Although grief is always unpleasant and uncomfortable, for some people certain aspects seem genuinely threatening. This perception can lead to attempts to control or avoid frightening feelings and reactions. For more on avoidance, see pages 78 and 81.

(2)

Your acute stress response is being triggered.

When something traumatic happens to you, your thoughts, emotions, and sensations at that moment can become paired with objects and other stimuli associated with the event. Later, when you encounter similar stimuli, it can trigger an acute stress response similar to what you experienced at the time of the trauma. This happens thanks to a well-known and well-researched phenomenon psychologists call *classical conditioning*.

Here's an example: a parent's phone rings at five a.m., and the person on the other end tells them that their son unexpectedly died in a car accident the night before. Before this moment, a phone ringing in the morning might not have given the parent a second thought, but now every time the phone rings before eight a.m., they feel a temporary surge of panic.

(3)

You fear the intensity of grief emotions.

After a loss, mourners often feel as though they are coming unhinged. If a person interprets their grief responses as dangerous, threatening, or indicative of a larger mental or physical problem, they are more likely to experience fear. Those who fear grief responses and grief-related emotions will likely experience increased anxiety when emotion feels unpredictable and easily triggered.

(4)

You feel as if you just now realized that bad things can happen anytime.

Before your loss, you may have assumed that the world was a place where things happened for a reason. You may have also subconsciously believed that bad things wouldn't happen to you. Since something bad *has* happened, you may now live with the anxiety that bad things can happen to anyone at any time. Some people have a tough time dealing with even the remote possibility of something terrible happening. You may have learned firsthand that worst-case, low-probability scenarios *can* happen. So even if the odds of an event occurring are slim, the mere uncertainty of whether or not it will happen is enough to cause intense anxiety and distress.

(5)

You don't want to find yourself caught off guard (again).

In 2011 Michelle Newman and Sandra Llera put forth a theory to explain worry and avoidance in generalized anxiety disorder called the *contrast-avoidance model*. They theorized that people use chronic worry in order to prevent themselves from experiencing a drastic increase in negative emotions in the event that something upsetting actually happens. If you think about it, our society promotes this mentality all the time. Think of common expressions such as "Brace yourself" and "Don't let your guard down," which translate to: "Don't let something bad happen when you least expect it."

(6)

You are experiencing an anxiety disorder, depression, or post-traumatic stress disorder.

Anxiety disorders are some of the most common mental health disorders. Logically, many people who already struggle with anxiety will experience grief at some time. For others, a loss may lead to new and unfamiliar struggles with anxiety. While it's normal to experience a sense of fear and apprehension during times of hardship and high stress, if you feel that you are experiencing excessive worry and panic for a prolonged period, it is a good idea to speak to a mental health professional.

OTHER LISTS TO CHECK OUT:

5 Realities of Acute Stress, page 74

5 Signs You Are Practicing Avoidance, page 81

4 Tips for Finding Calm In Your Grief Storm, page 203

5

Reactions You May Have to a Chaotic and Uncontrollable World

For many people, an experience with loss is the first time they've felt flung around by the fickle finger of fate. Suffering at the hands of forces that you neither expected nor provoked can leave you struggling with the sense that life is erratic, unpredictable, unjust, and filled with danger. How you respond to this perception has a lot to do with things we've already discussed, like fear and anxiety. So keep what you've learned about these things in mind as you consider these common responses to feeling a sense of chaos and uncontrollability.

(1)

You may try to control everything.

When a person feels genuinely helpless and vulnerable for the first time, they may respond by trying to control everything—like their environment, emotions, family, and friends. They think the more control they have, the better they can protect themselves and those they love (overprotective parenting is an example of this). But here's the problem—some things are simply out of everyone's control. It's impossible to prevent *any and all* future negative experiences, and trying to do so is an all-consuming full-time job.

(2)
You may want to give up.

On the other end of the spectrum, some people may think they have less ability to influence their environment than they previously believed. *Learned helplessness* is a phenomenon that occurs when a person passively gives up trying because they think bad things will happen regardless of their actions. For example, someone exposed to multiple traumas and losses may stop trying to cope with pain and may give up on efforts to seek solutions or improve their situation. They may ask, "What's the point of doing these things if I'm just going to be knocked down again?"

(3)
You may blame yourself or others for the loss.

The idea that bad things happen for senseless reasons is unacceptable for some. So naturally, many will look for reasons to explain what's happened. Though it's possible to find meaning that leads to a sense of comfort, many people find more distressing and problematic explanations for what's happened, like blaming oneself or someone else for the loss. This kind of blame feels bad, but for some, living with the belief that bad things happen at random feels worse.

(4)
You may lose trust in others.

Few of us can always be in charge all the time. In many scenarios, we must hand over control to the person in charge (think: airplane pilots or surgeons). And to feel safe in these instances, one must have a sense of trust in the person at the helm.

After a loss, a person may feel harmed or let down by those they trusted to keep them safe. In some instances, you may also feel abused, exploited, or abandoned. Other times, you may simply realize the person you put your faith in is just as fallible and incapable of preventing harm as you are. In any of these instances, one may experience diminished trust in others and be less willing to hand over control in the future.

(5)

You may seek control through ritual.

It may surprise you to hear that rituals are connected to control. To understand the connection, let's look at superstition, which is an everyday type of ritual. We know that wearing lucky socks doesn't win championship games and screaming into the freezer doesn't cause snow days, but people do these things anyway. People engage in superstitions because they want to feel like they have some control in achieving a desired outcome, despite knowing, in many cases, that the events they're trying to influence have little to do with them.

Superstitions aside, there's research to indicate that grief-related rituals might help to provide a sense of control. Researchers Michael Norton and Francesca Gino (2013, 2014) found in their studies that engaging in rituals provided bereaved individuals a sense of control in situations in which they otherwise felt helpless and powerless.

OTHER LISTS TO CHECK OUT:

6 Causes of Grief-Related Anxiety, page 84

3 Existential Questions Prompted by Loss, page 148

7 Steps to Help You Live According to Your Values, page 167

5

FAQs About Yearning

Yearning is the part of grief responsible for the missing, longing, aching, and wishing to put things back the way they were. It feels like wanting reunification with someone or something so badly that your heart is clawing out of your chest trying to grab ahold of the past. Even if it's just for one hour, you would give anything to go back and feel what life was like before, to bring your two-dimensional memories to life with vivid details. Like many things in grief, the experience of yearning is subjective. But there are a few questions we can answer with a bit of certainty.

How is yearning defined?

1

In German there is a word, *sehnsucht*, which can be defined as "a high degree or intense (recurring) and often painful desire for something, particularly if there is no hope to attain the desired, or when its attainment is uncertain, still far away" (Grimm and Grimm, 1984). Although there isn't an exact English translation, we think *sehnsucht* accurately illustrates the intense and ongoing emotional state of yearning. Regarding yearning after loss, we like this description from Mary-Frances O'Connor and Tamara Sussman (2014): "an emotional state widely experienced in situations involving loss, focused on a desire for a person, place, or thing that was treasured in the past."

(2) What types of losses are associated with yearning?

All losses may be associated with yearning, especially when one longs for something in the past. Even when the loss involves troubled relationships or painful experiences, you may still yearn for better times that preceeded the loss. A few examples of losses that tend to cause yearning include:

- Grieving the death of a loved one
- Breakups and estrangements
- Aging, mourning the past, and the passage of time
- Grieving for a home, whether a house or a town or country
- Longing for the time before illness or injury, when things seemed simpler
- Retirement
- Children going off to college

(3) How common is yearning?

Very! In fact, yearning is one of the most common grief responses after a loved one's death. If you're surprised to hear that, you're not alone—most people associate sadness and depressed mood with grief. However, research with bereaved individuals has shown that yearning is in fact the most frequently reported psychological response (Zhang et al. 2007).

(4)

Is yearning technically a feeling?

It's complicated. Like many experiences, yearning has a cognitive (thinking) component and an affective (feeling) component. Thoughts related to yearning may involve imagining what life would be like and how you and your relationship would differ if the loss hadn't occurred.

(5)

Is yearning good or bad?

Neither—or both, depending on how you look at it. Yearning can certainly feel distressing because you long for something only to find, over and over again, that it's gone. In other words, you're repeatedly reminded of your loss.

That said, yearning has positive attributes as well. One of the reasons people reminisce is because it feels good to remember. Though nostalgia is a phenomenon by a different name, it shares many of the same features as yearning. Nostalgia, which is conceptualized as a "primarily positive experience colored with some bittersweet elements," has been shown to counteract negative psychological and physiological states. When people feel sad, stressed, or lonely, they may access memories from the past to make themselves feel better. Memories of happier times balance out more distressing thoughts and emotions (Zhou 2012).

OTHER LISTS TO CHECK OUT:

6 Mixed-Up Emotions You May Feel in Loss, page 70
4 Reasons to Love the Concept of Continuing Bonds, page 259
20 Ways to Connect with Memories, page 268

5

Facts About Rumination

When we ask people about their common grief experience, rumination isn't usually at the top of the list. But the moment we describe it we're met with instant looks of recognition. Rumination is surprisingly common, though it often goes unnamed. Though there are different definitions of rumination floating around out there, for our purposes we will use a psychological definition of grief rumination put forth by Maarten Eisma and Margaret Stroebe: "repetitive and recurrent thinking about causes and consequences of the loss and loss-related emotions" (Eisma and Stroebe, 2017).

If you've ever found your brain turning the causes and consequences of your loss round and round, never making much progress, you've ruminated. This brooding can have negative effects, so let's talk through some details.

①

Rumination after a loss (in small doses) is not a problem.

Repetitive thinking about something painful sounds like a problem, we know. But at its core, rumination is thinking really deeply about something difficult that's happened to you. After a loss, especially an unexpected one, your brain tries to process and make sense of an event that disrupted your life in a significant way. It is no surprise that it would do some replaying of the causes and consequences as it tries to construct a narrative about what happened. Within limits, that's actually normal.

(2)

In fact, most people engage in some rumination.

When a behavior has negative connotations or consequences (and rumination does), people tend to assume it is abnormal. But in the days or weeks following a loss, it is common for people to rehash what happened, playing those causes and consequences over and over. It's common enough that grief therapists have a validated grief rumination scale to measure this behavior when people come into grief counseling (Eisma et al., 2014).

(3)

Rumination should dissipate with time.

Slowly, as your brain accepts the reality of what has happened and makes logical sense of those particulars, the rumination often quiets down. This doesn't mean you'll never have a bad night overthinking the specifics of your divorce or replaying the moments before your sister's death. It also doesn't mean you won't occasionally find new things to ruminate about. As you navigate life after loss, worry is common. Sometimes that worry will briefly turn into rumination. You just want to keep an eye out if it becomes persistent.

(4)

Rumination can definitely become a problem (a big problem, at that).

We don't want to scare you if you find yourself in a rumination cycle at the moment, but we do want to be clear—rumination can become incredibly problematic. Don't believe us? Researchers at Yale University who've spent a long time investigating the ins and outs of rumination have found good evidence that rumination "exacerbates depression, enhances negative thinking, impairs problem-solving, interferes with instrumental behavior, and erodes social support" (Nolen-Hoeksema, 2008). Yikes. Don't worry, we've got a coping list to help you if you're worried your rumination is out of hand (see page 213).

$$\text{⑤}$$

Rumination in grief is a form of avoidance.

We know—this is completely counterintuitive. As we talked about on page 78, avoidance is when you work hard not to think about something. Rumination is when you repetitively think about something. How could rumination possibly be a form of avoidance? Margaret Stroebe, Henk Schut, Maarten Eisma, and an array of their colleagues first suggested this "rumination as avoidance" hypothesis and then did research to investigate it. There is a lot to say on this topic, but here's what you need to know: studies have found that grieving people will often ruminate on very specific aspects of their loss. This keeps their brains so busy with those very focused events or details that they don't have to face the even more difficult and painful aspects of their grief.

OTHER LISTS TO CHECK OUT:

9 Practices to Help You Reduce Worry and Rumination, page 213
6 Suggestions for Living with Guilt and Regret, page 218
4 Places to Look for Grief Support in Your Community, page 256

4

Realities About Relief

The American Psychological Association defines relief as "a positive emotion that occurs as a response to a threat that has abated, disappeared, or failed to materialize." This definition makes relief sound pretty simple, and quite often, it is. But that's not always true, especially not in grief. Though relief is a common response to loss, it's also typical for relief to cause guilt and confusion. Let's clarify some of the most common misconceptions about this feeling.

①

When do people feel relief in grief?

Some losses, though certainly not all, follow a period of suffering. It might have been a rocky marriage, a difficult job, or a prolonged period of mental or physical illness before a death. Whether this period of suffering was brief or protracted, it likely created anxiety or distress. The loss, though devastating, put an end to that suffering, which brought the very normal and very natural feeling of relief.

②

So relief means I'm glad the loss happened?

No! You're glad that *the suffering ended*, not glad about how the suffering was brought to an end. If you could choose, you would likely have picked an alternate ending: your loved one would have recovered fully from their illness; you and your partner would have found a way to both be happy in your relationship; your workplace issues would have been seamlessly resolved. Unfortunately, we don't usually get to pick the ending.

③
But at least relief makes grief easier, right?

Nope, sorry. Relief is part of your grief. It doesn't reduce the complex pain of life after loss. Though you may feel grateful that your suffering or the suffering of the person you love has ended, that doesn't magically make the gaping hole left in your life any smaller. Ending the suffering you experienced before the loss doesn't ease the anguish you feel after the loss.

④
If relief is normal and natural, why do I feel so guilty about it?

If you're struggling with relief-induced guilt, you are not alone. Often that guilt comes from misunderstanding what relief means (and what it doesn't). Let's recap: the relief means you're glad that suffering has ended. That is not only normal, it's compassionate. Relief does *not* mean that you're glad that someone died, your marriage failed, or you lost your job.

OTHER LISTS TO CHECK OUT:

4 Things You Can Do to Cope with Conflicting Emotions, page 193

6 Mixed-Up Emotions You May Feel in Loss, page 70

5 Realities of Acute Stress, page 74

3

Questions About Feeling Nothing

One can feel so many things in this life—anger, joy, jealousy, love, shame, happiness, embarrassment, amusement, sadness, euphoria, frustration. The roller coaster of emotion whips over high peaks, spins, and dips, over and over again. It's thrilling, and it's scary, and it's one hell of a ride.

Except now, imagine that one day you get on the roller coaster, and as it climbs, falls, twists, and turns, you realize that you feel nothing. Instead, you are sitting in a tiny cart being whipped around like a wet noodle, wondering why everyone else is laughing and throwing their hands in the air.

1 IS THERE A WORD FOR "FEELING NOTHING"?

The technical word for feeling nothing is *anhedonia*. Anhedonia is one of the main symptoms of major depressive disorder. Someone might also experience this sort of reaction in response to loss, anxiety, or trauma. Anhedonia can be described as the inability to feel pleasure or a loss of interest in previously rewarding or enjoyable activities such as hobbies, work, food, sex, and laughing. However, some might say this description pales in comparison to the real thing.

2 WHAT DOES FEELING NOTHING *FEEL* LIKE?

Feeling nothing is not akin to feeling "okay," underwhelmed, or unenthused. Feeling nothing is more like feeling empty, dead inside, emotionless, as though you have nothing to contribute, or like you can't relate to the feelings and emotions of others.

It's hard to understand how the absence of feeling can actually equal extreme pain and distress, but it does. When you feel nothing, the world makes less sense. You look in the mirror and barely recognize yourself; without emotions, you feel alien, and it's hard to imagine being a person ever again. The emotional numbness sometimes experienced in grief can feel especially disturbing because you *expect* to feel so much more.

3 IS FEELING NOTHING NORMAL?

It's normal to feel numb or unemotional at points in your grief; this does not reflect anything negative about you as a person.

Like most experiences, feeling nothing exists on a continuum. It's normal to feel numb at times, but if you feel nothing for a *long time*, it could signal a significant issue. If you've felt this way for longer than you're comfortable with, you may want to speak with a licensed mental health professional.

OTHER LISTS TO CHECK OUT:

Make Your Own List: What Are Your Grief Emotions?, page 68
5 Realities of Acute Stress, page 74
7 Steps to Help You Cope When You Don't Feel Like Coping, page 196

4

Reasons Guilt Is Even More Complicated Than You Think

Though guilt is a remarkably common grief emotion, it remains one of the trickiest to navigate. Guilt can make others uncomfortable and dismissive. You wouldn't be the first to express your guilt only to be met with, "Oh, you shouldn't feel guilty. Just let that go, it wasn't your fault." Though whoever dismissed your guilt was probably well-intentioned, no one likes being told their feelings are wrong. More than that, you likely won't stop feeling guilty because someone told you to. That isn't how feelings work.

Let's get one thing straight: it is okay to feel guilty. Really. But it's also important to then understand, examine, and cope with that guilt.

①

There is no single definition of guilt.

If you were to comb through the mental health literature, you'd notice that there is no one definition of guilt. In fact, a 2010 review of dozens of psychological definitions and measures of guilt found that "definitions were highly diverse and did not conceptually converge on a common underlying construct" (Tilghman-Osborne, 2010).

Most people generally agree that guilt is the emotional response you have after committing a (real or perceived) moral transgression. Put simply, when you think you have done something wrong, you feel guilty.

(2)

Thinking you did something wrong doesn't mean you actually *did*.

Your thoughts and feelings are not always accurate. Let us say that again. *Your thoughts and feelings are not always accurate.* Sometimes, you feel guilty because you actually did something wrong, harmful, or hurtful. But sometimes you feel guilty because you merely *think* you did something wrong, harmful, or hurtful. Just because you feel guilty doesn't mean you are guilty. We'll remind you of this again in our list about coping with guilt (see page 218).

(3)

Guilt and *regret* are often used interchangeably, but they are not the same thing.

Colloquially, these words are often used interchangeably. But the distinction between guilt and regret is useful in understanding your emotional experience. Guilt is the feeling that you've done something you knew was wrong, harmful, or hurtful. Regret, on the other hand, is simply the emotion felt when you look back and wish you had done something differently or that an outcome had been different. They are related emotions, but the distinction is consequential. When a person feels regret, they may quickly start to blame themselves before investigating what they could actually control. Though guilt almost always involves regret, regret doesn't always involve guilt. Ultimately, clarifying whether you feel guilt, regret, or both is critical when figuring out how to cope with these complex emotions.

(4)

Guilt can leave you in an endless cycle of "coulda, woulda, shoulda."

When you feel tremendous guilt, it can put you in a rumination loop, cycling through every decision you made and action you took. Once you've decided something was your fault, it can be hard to recognize any evidence to the contrary. And even if it was your fault, the path to self-forgiveness and self-compassion can be incredibly hard to find on your own. We have some suggestions for coping with guilt on page 218, but this is an area where professional support may be a big help.

OTHER LISTS TO CHECK OUT:

6 Suggestions for Living with Guilt and Regret, page 218

9 Suggestions for Finding Self-Forgiveness (and Making Amends), page 223

8 Misconceptions About Blame, Anger, and Forgiveness, page 244

5

Questions About Shame and Stigma

Imagine that your sense of self and identity are a protective suit of armor that you wear throughout life, shielding you from threats to your self-perception and other emotional injuries.

For example, let's say that part of your identity includes the certainty that you're a good friend. If someone tells you you're a terrible friend, you probably won't believe them. You may wonder whether you did something hurtful to them, but most likely, you won't generalize this to contradict your belief about yourself.

Though some people's armor is more permeable than others, we all have weak spots, especially after a loss. When we say that loss can shatter a person's world, we include your inner world, where your identity, self-worth, beliefs, and value system live. And feeling less self-assured, confused, overwhelmed, and uncertain may make you especially vulnerable to attacks on your sense of self—specifically, those that come in the form of stigma, self-stigma, and shame.

①

What is stigma?

Simply put, a stigma is a negative impression held toward someone based on a distinguishing trait, characteristic, or circumstance (for example, stigmatizing attitudes towards people with mental health conditions). Stigma may include attitudes and judgments that create shame, disgrace, stereo-types, and prejudice.

(2)
How is stigma connected to grief?

After loss, people may experience stigma for many reasons, but we'd like to focus on two significant causes. First, a person may feel stigmatized for their loss, such as if someone suggests that the loss was their fault or their choice. If the loss is death-related, a person may also feel their deceased loved one is being judged or blamed. This is common when a loved one dies a substance-related death or by suicide.

Second, a person may feel *their grief* is being stigmatized. Unfortunately, family, friends, and random strangers have all kinds of opinions about other people's grief, including that:

- the person's grieving too much, too little, or too long
- the person's grief is a sign of weakness
- the person's emotion is unacceptable or bothersome
- the person isn't entitled to grieve the loss in the first place

(3)
What is self-stigma?

According to Patrick Corrigan and Deepa Rao (2012), "Public stigma refers to the negative attitudes held by members of the public about people with devalued characteristics. Self-stigma occurs when people internalize these public attitudes and suffer numerous negative consequences as a result."

In other words, whether someone has expressed a negative attitude to-ward you or not, you know such an attitude exists. Some attitudes you dismiss. Others you may buy into, internalize, and apply to yourself and your experiences.

4

Why would anyone believe negative things about themselves?

Let us remind you, your armor is tattered and torn. Even if you've never felt vulnerable to specific attacks on your character or identity before, you may now find self-doubt subtly creeping in. Also, there are other reasons for grief-related self-stigma, including:

- **Attitudes you formed before the loss:** People go into grief with already developed beliefs and attitudes about loss, grief, and coping. Some of these beliefs may help a person's suffering, and some may reflect negative attitudes and stereotypes.
- **Negative messages:** If a person receives negative comments from others about their loss, a loved one's death, or their grief frequently enough, they may begin to agree with them.
- **Blame, guilt, shame, regret, and fear of emotion:** Many common and natural grief reactions can compound or affirm negative beliefs about who is to blame, who is deserving of sympathy, and who is responsible.

5

How does shame relate to grief?

In her 2004 study, "Shame Resilience Theory: A Grounded Theory Study on Women and Shame," Brené Brown described shame as

"an intensely painful feeling or experience of believing we are flawed and therefore unworthy of acceptance and belonging."

Other simple ways to describe shame include embarrassment or the sense that you are flawed or "bad." Shame is often lumped in with guilt, but it's important to note the two are not the same. While guilt is focused on an action (*What I did was terrible*), shame is focused on oneself (*I am terrible*). Guilt can, however, trigger a sense of shame when it affirms what a person already suspected about themselves (*I betrayed my friend because I am a bad person*).

The same forces that work to stigmatize and self-stigmatize also create shame. A few grief-specific factors might include the following.

- You feel you're to blame, responsible, or deserving of the loss.
- You are ashamed of how you responded at the time of the loss. You may feel you betrayed your morals or beliefs or that you let others down.
- You believe the loss proves negative things about you, such as that you're weak, unlovable, incapable, or irresponsible.
- You feel ashamed of your grief. You worry that you can't handle it, that you're abnormal, or that people are tired of your suffering.

OTHER LISTS TO CHECK OUT

6 Suggestions for Living with Guilt and Regret, page 218

Make Your Own List: What's Your Grief Secret?, page 110

9 Suggestions for Finding Self-Forgiveness (and Making Amends), page 223

10

Types of Stigmatizing Statements

We hope that harsh remarks and careless responses toward grieving people are outliers. But we know a negative experience can leave a far more lasting impression than a positive one. And remember, the seeds of stigma are embedded in the beliefs and attitudes we perceive from friends, family, community members, and society at large. This list of grief-related statements demonstrates the types of comments that can lead to disenfranchisement, isolation, stigma, self-stigma, and shame. Of note: these examples are real comments shared with us by our online community.

1 STATEMENTS THAT IMPLY BLAME
"What did you think was going to happen? He was a drug addict!"

2 STATEMENTS THAT INSPIRE SHAME
"Don't be depressed. No one likes people who are depressed."

3 STATEMENTS THAT MINIMIZE THE LOSS
"It's not a big deal because, literally, everyone dies."

4 STATEMENTS THAT DIMINISH THE IMPORTANCE OF THE LOSS
"You can always remarry."

5 STATEMENTS THAT DISCOURAGE GRIEF
"I am going to hang up now—call me back when you stop crying."

6 STATEMENTS THAT DISCOURAGE STAYING CONNECTED
"I don't want to sound mean, but you need to move on. She's gone."

7 STATEMENTS THAT MAKE GRIEF SEEM ABNORMAL OR UNHEALTHY
"Why are you still grieving? It's almost been a year!"

8 STATEMENTS THAT BYPASS PAIN
"Don't be sad when there's so much to be grateful for."

9 STATEMENTS THAT PUT UNDUE PRESSURE ON THE PERSON
"You have to be strong. You're the man of the house now."

10 STATEMENTS THAT IMPLY WEAKNESS
"Stop feeling sorry for yourself, you're being selfish."

OTHER LISTS TO CHECK OUT:

What's Your Grief Secret?

"When we keep a secret, that secret is actually keeping us . . . maybe haunting us, maybe inviting us to reconcile with part of our past we're hiding from, maybe keeping us from having intimate relationships with others or ourselves."

—FRANK WARREN, CREATOR OF POSTSECRET

Do you have a grief secret that you keep hidden out of fear of shame, judgment, or guilt? If so, you're not alone. Grief secrets are remarkably common. Inspired by the project PostSecret, What's Your Grief started a Grief Secret project in 2019, and since then we've received hundreds of anonymous submissions.

What would happen if you let your grief secret out somehow? Seriously, consider it. People have rational reasons for keeping things private. However, we also know that many people hold on to secrets despite any evidence that they will have real-world consequences.

A series of studies conducted at the University of Notre Dame found that people benefited from the insights they gained by revealing their secrets. One such study even pointed to the possibility that revealing secrets to an accepting, discreet confidant decreases alienation and benefits physical health (Kelly et al, 2001). So despite what you may fear about revealing your secrets, there is real reason to believe it could help.

Secrets are scariest when you keep them tucked away and unexamined. By doing so, you never have the chance to prove them wrong or learn that people will still like and love you even if the secrets are true. Many times, when you let the sinister secret out into the light you realize it was only frightening when shrouded in darkness. Furthermore, keeping secrets keeps *you* in hiding, which wastes mental and emotional energy. And both are in short supply when you're grieving.

We won't ask you to shout your secrets for all to hear. We believe sharing your secret with someone—perhaps a trusted friend or a therapist—can help you receive vital support and connect with others. But we realize this is a pretty giant leap for some. Instead, we're going to ask you to take one small step by acknowledging your grief secret(s) in a safe way.

So here's what we want you to do:

- Get out a sheet of paper or a journal and write down your grief secrets (even if you can only come up with one). These could be thoughts, memories, or beliefs about yourself, your loved ones, your loss, or your grief that you've been avoiding.

- After writing your secret(s) down, ask yourself:

  - How does it feel to acknowledge a thought you've been avoiding?

  - What do you believe this secret says about you?

  - Has this secret prevented you from connecting with other people?

  - Has this secret prevented you from processing or coping with a particular aspect of your grief or life after loss?

  - Who is one person you would consider sharing this secret with? Think about someone who would be accepting, nonjudgmental, and discreet. What would happen if you shared this secret with them?

8

Feelings That Can Make Grief Ugly, Mean, or Messy

Society has created this narrative that idealizes the idea of grieving with grace. You have probably seen it in the movies, in books, and subtly being reinforced when people compliment you on how strong you are and how you are handling things with such poise. Poise . . . blech.

As annoying as this narrative is, we understand why it persists. It is far more comfortable to imagine that coping with life's losses can be tidy and controlled instead of ugly and messy.

It isn't easy to be open about all the mucky, chaotic stuff if you feel pressure to only display that strong, graceful ideal. You may feel like your grief should be a single tear running down your stoic cheek as you gaze off toward the horizon. In reality, your grief feels more like a blotchy, swollen, snotty, red face over a pint of Ben and Jerry's next to a growing mountain of dirty laundry.

Here's a little list to remind you of the reality that grief isn't always strong, courageous, graceful, or poised. Grief feelings are often messy, complicated, and ugly and sometimes make you feel like you're a bad person.

Chances are you are none of these things.

1

You feel jealous of people you love.

You might know this as, "I want to be happy that you're happy, but instead I just feel kind of bitter and resentful." Your best friend gets her dream job as you're still reeling after being laid off. It isn't that you aren't happy for her somewhere deep down, you're just having a hard time finding it.

2

You feel entitled, like life owes you something.

Just about anytime anything bad happens. You get pulled over for speeding; doesn't this cop know your husband just died?

3

You don't care about anything.

Every single thing at work, every single day.

4

You are having thoughts about suicide.

You lie in bed and think, "Man, it sure would be easier if I just didn't wake up tomorrow." It is estimated that approximately twelve million Americans have serious thoughts of suicide each year (SAMHSA, 2020). It doesn't mean you're crazy. It does mean it's important to talk to a professional, so those thoughts don't spiral. If you're having thoughts of suicide, find the suicide hotline number and other resources on page 275.

5

You are angry. SO. ANGRY.

You are angry at the person who died. You're angry at your ex for rejecting you. You're angry at your boss for laying you off. You are angry at your family for how bad they are at supporting you. You are angry at people for asking how you are doing. You are angry at people for not asking how you are doing. You are angry at God for taking your loved one. You are angry at yourself for not being strong and poised. You get the idea.

6

You're numb.

You've lost your job, you're at risk of losing your house to foreclosure, yet you feel absolutely nothing. You can't remember the last time you felt a feeling. You're convinced something must be wrong with you. Don't panic. Turns out our brains do this self-protectively sometimes. If this lasts more than a few weeks, you may want to talk to someone. But don't worry, you're still human.

7

You feel out of control.

You can't focus on anything. You are snapping at your roommate. You cry every time you get in the car (what is it about the car?). This is shockingly normal. Most people don't have experience tolerating the tornado of emotions that come up all at once after a loss. It takes practice.

You are judging other people, even people you care about.

You're barely keeping your head above the grief water, and meanwhile your friends are busy talking to you about house hunting and how the dry cleaner lost their favorite coat. You can't help but think they have absolutely no idea what is truly important in life. Don't worry, you're not a bad person. People's values and priorities often change after big losses and life transitions, which isn't always a bad thing. Usually this settles down. You will probably eventually be able to listen to friends vent about how hard life has been since the drive-through Starbucks in their neighborhood closed. And the good news is that many people who experience this change in priorities feel it has helped them grow.

OTHER LISTS TO CHECK OUT:

6 Things to Understand About Anger, page 127

3 Questions About Feeling Nothing, page 99

6 Ways Grief Can Change Your Priorities, page 145

7

Common Defense Mechanisms Explained

Sigmund Freud (the founder of psychoanalysis and the one name you likely remember from Psych 101), first discussed defense mechanisms in his 1894 paper "The Neuro-Psychoses of Defence." Since that introduction he, his daughter, Anna Freud, and many other psychologists have expanded on the concept and utilized it to understand specific behaviors.

Defense mechanisms are behaviors used to protect oneself from unpleasant thoughts and emotions that cause anxiety and threaten one's sense of self. We all use them from time to time, but we usually don't realize it because a key feature of defense mechanisms is that they happen below the surface of our conscious mind, in the unconscious.

One way to think of defense mechanisms is like a little man working as a bouncer at the door to your consciousness. He takes his job very seriously, and that job is to fill your conscious mind with thoughts and feelings that make you comfortable. So when uncomfortable thoughts and feelings like guilt, anger, shame, blame, jealousy, or inferiority try to enter your awareness, the bouncer uses a defense mechanism to keep them out.

The idea that your unconscious is shielding you from your own thoughts and emotions might leave you with a sense of powerlessness. How are you ever supposed to truly know yourself without all that information? Don't worry; defense mechanisms aren't perfect filters.

Your true feelings are often accessible if you engage in introspection about what exists both on and below the surface. And though defense mechanisms may be triggered without much conscious thought, they result in conscious behaviors that you can easily identify if you know what you're looking for.

Although there are many defense mechanisms, we will only mention a handful here that relate to grief.

1 · Denial

Denial is used to avoid acknowledging an unpleasant truth or reality, usually because the reality is painful or threatening. There is no end to the ways that a person can use denial in their grief. Examples include saying and believing things like, "I don't need help," "I'm fine," "I don't have a problem," "Nothing needs to change," or "I'm over it."

2 · Regression

Who hasn't had a good grief temper tantrum? We sure have. When a person uses regression, they revert to an earlier stage of development and display what might look like immature and insecure behavior. An adult engaging in regression during grief might shut down or withdraw, become clingy with family and friends, or act childish.

3 · Projection

Projection is when a person has thoughts and feelings that they believe are unacceptable, but instead of acknowledging them, they attribute them to someone else. For example, you're mad at your friend, but you don't want to *admit* you're mad, so instead you project your feelings onto them by saying, "I know you're mad at me. Why are you mad at me?"

4 · Displacement

Displacement is when a person has thoughts and emotions toward someone or something, but instead of directing them toward the appropriate source, they take them out on another person or object. This defense mechanism is often used when a person cannot express their emotions toward the true source because doing so would be ineffectual or have negative consequences.

Quite often, grieving people have strong feelings toward faith, illness, death, grief, the person who died, or the person they blame for the death. In many of these instances, they can't take their emotions out on the source, so instead they displace them onto someone or something else.

5 · Intellectualization

When a person is confronted with painful or frightening emotions, they might try to intellectualize, or rationalize, them rather than experience them. They may do this by reading a lot, learning about their experiences, or overanalyzing their thoughts and emotions. In this way, the person avoids confronting their feelings by examining them at arm's length.

6 · Undoing

When a person has behaved negatively toward someone or had unpleasant thoughts about that person, they may feel guilt. Afterward, they may try to *undo* their behavior by engaging in opposite actions or thoughts.

Undoing can play a role in grief in many ways. For example, people commonly feel guilty for the negative things they said or did toward deceased loved ones in the past. So they go out of their way to say only wonderful things about the deceased after they're gone.

7 · Sublimation

Sublimation is when a person channels their painful and threatening experiences into positive or acceptable outlets. We see examples of sublimation time and time again in grief when people use their experiences to create, educate, advocate, and support others.

OTHER LISTS TO CHECK OUT:

6 Causes of Grief-Related Anxiety, page 84

8 Feelings That Can Make Grief Ugly, Mean, or Messy, page 112

4 Mind Tricks That Complicate Grief, page 120

4

Mind Tricks That Complicate Grief

Your brain is a busy machine. Since your loss, you may feel like it's on a constant coffee break, but it's still working very hard in ways you don't realize. The senses gather roughly eleven million bits of information per second from the environment, and you're only ever aware of a tiny percentage of that. So a vast majority of processing is happening outside the conscious mind, which sometimes results in the formation of biases, assumptions, and other errors in thinking.

We've identified four biases and ways of thinking that can have considerable influence on your judgment and perceptions. Although they represent normal ways of thinking, in grief they can sometimes cause more harm than good.

1 · Confirmation Bias

Confirmation bias describes the tendency to selectively pay attention to and remember evidence that bolsters your belief, while also ignoring contradictory evidence. When you're grieving, you're already predisposed to think negatively about the world and the people in it. Then confirmation bias comes in and makes things worse by pointing out all the ways in which you're right. So perhaps when laying your head down at night, you don't remember the neighbor who smiled at you and said, "Good morning!" or the driver who let you switch lanes in traffic, but you do remember the person who cut you off in line at your local coffee joint.

2 · Magical Thinking

Magical thinking is the belief that one's thoughts or words can cause events or outcomes that, in reality, they cannot influence. An everyday example of magical thinking would be the hesitancy to discuss a potential outcome out loud because you don't want to jinx it. Or, after mentioning the possibility of a future unpleasant event, feeling the need to knock on wood to prevent it from happening.

Magical thinking is common in young children approximately ages 2 to 7. At this age, children are still exploring cause-and-effect relationships and have yet to fully grasp how their thoughts, desires, and actions relate to the outside world. Thanks to magical thinking, children often believe their thoughts and wishes can affect what happens in real life. For example, a child who wishes for a younger sibling may believe they are to thank when they find out their mother is expecting.

Unfortunately, magical thinking can have confusing consequences for grieving children who believe their thoughts or wishes are to blame for their loss. For example, a boy who said he wished he didn't have such a mean father in a moment of anger may later feel responsible when his parents split up and his father moves out. Also, a child may believe that he can reverse his loss by wishing for things to go back the way they were.

Sadly, a child who constructs a magical-thinking type of explanation for events may live with the burden of guilt, blame, and shame for reasons adults would never even consider. In time, these children should develop the logic to understand their magical thinking was flawed. However, because our thoughts and emotions aren't always rational, these individuals may continue to live with feelings of responsibility into adulthood.

But magical thinking isn't just something kids do. To quote Joan Didion, who wrote about her own grief in her memoir *The Year of Magical Thinking*: "I was thinking as small children think, as if my thoughts or wishes had the power to reverse the narrative." Although adults may logically understand their thoughts can't prevent or reverse their losses, many people behave as though they can. For example, they punish themselves for "causing" events that they realistically have no responsibility for.

3 · Hindsight Bias

It may be hard for you to believe this, because you now know how things turned out, but you didn't *really* know as much as you think you did in the past. You may have worried or had your suspicions, but you didn't *know*. Or if you did know, the things you think you could have done differently weren't quite as apparent to you then as they seem now. We know this because you are looking at things in hindsight, and hindsight is biased.

Hindsight bias is a normal and common psychological phenomenon that causes people to believe that past outcomes were predictable. When looking at events afterward, people tend to notice information that is consistent with what they now know to be true. The same tendency causes them to ignore neutral or contradictory evidence (yes, a little like confirmation bias!).

Ultimately, when a person tries to piece together a meaningful narrative after their loss, as people are wont to do, they wind up with a story that goes: *this was the beginning, here were the signs, here's where things went wrong, and this is the outcome.*

For some, it is comforting to create a narrative that brings order to the confusing chaos of death and grief, and many people find reassuring answers to questions like "Why?" and "What went wrong?" But on the other end of the spectrum, many people construct a narrative that causes them to feel unpleasant things like guilt, blame, shame, regret, and personal responsibility.

4 · Counterfactual Thinking

When you ask questions like "What if?" and "What might have been?" you are engaging in counterfactual thinking. Counterfactual thinking is the act of coming up with alternative outcomes counter to (or different from) the facts. Some examples:

- "If I hadn't slept late, I wouldn't have missed the bus."
- "If I had gone to that party like I wanted, then I wouldn't have aced my math test."

One can see how counterfactual thinking can have negative implications for a person who is grieving, especially when combined with hindsight bias. Through a narrative constructed using hindsight bias, one might believe that other, more preferable counterfactual realities would have been the reality if only they'd done something different. Even though one can come up with many counterfactual realities in any situation, and there's little way of knowing if any might have come to fruition, grieving people commonly struggle with guilt and blame based on these hypothetical outcomes.

OTHER LISTS TO CHECK OUT:

7 Common Defense Mechanisms Explained, page 116

6 Suggestions for Living with Guilt and Regret, page 218

16 Questions to Help You Understand Your Grief Story, page 282

5

Sources of
Grief-Related Stress

"No one ever told me that grief felt so like fear."

—C. S. LEWIS, *A GRIEF OBSERVED*

In their 1984 book, *Stress, Appraisal, and Coping*, Richard S. Lazarus and Susan Folkman explained that humans make two appraisals when responding to stress: a primary appraisal and a secondary appraisal.

In the *primary appraisal*, a person evaluates whether the potential stressor is relevant to them. They determine if the circumstances affect them, and if so, how. If the person feels the stressor is relevant, they then decide if it is also threatening. This assessment is subjective and may be based on whether the stressor impacts their time, resources, relationships, or physical or mental well-being. When a stressor is determined to be both relevant and threatening, a person experiences stress. Then, the person makes a secondary appraisal about their ability to cope. The fewer resources the person determines they have to deal with the threat, the more stress they will experience.

Spelled out like this, the experience of stress seems very deliberate and formulaic. As someone who's experienced stress, you know that's not typically how things go down. This sequence of appraisals happens very quickly and often without your conscious awareness. For example, if you come face to face with a grizzly bear in the woods, you're not going to engage in a protracted analysis. Your stress response will kick in fast because your brain and body have all the information they need to appraise the stressor. Bears are dangerous, big, and fast. While you, no offense, are less big and less fast.

When you experienced loss, your immediate stress response may have felt like the equivalent of meeting a bear in the woods. (See page 74 for a more in-depth discussion of the acute stress response). Since then, you've likely been exposed to persistent stressors due to secondary losses, adapting to life after loss, and your ongoing grief. Repeated exposure to stressors like these is called *chronic stress*.

An important first step in coping with stress is understanding the role it plays in your life. Consider how your grief and loss manifest in the following common sources of stress.

1 · Change

Many people find after loss that they have to adjust to a life that looks nothing like it used to. As you've discovered, one significant loss can cause a ripple effect of secondary losses. The number of factors that may change as a result is endless. Even good changes—such as graduation, having a child, or retirement—can cause significant amounts of loss and stress.

2 · Emotions

A key factor contributing to a person's subjective experience of stress is whether they believe they have the resources or know-how to cope with the stressor. Experiences like trauma, loss, and grief can evoke new and intense emotions that people often feel ill-equipped to deal with.

3 · Interpersonal stressors

Sadly, tension and interpersonal conflict are common after loss. Conflict and strain can arise when close friends and family don't understand the significance of a person's grief or fail to offer adequate support. Also, misunderstanding and hurt feelings are common among people who are grieving the same loss when everyone struggles to deal with the loss in their own unique way.

4 · Pressure

It would be wonderful if people could take time off from their responsibilities and obligations after loss, perhaps long enough to allow them to process their emotions, cope with logistical issues, and maybe get their lives together. Sadly, loss doesn't exist in a bubble, and grieving people often feel immense pressure to feel better, support others, get back to "normal," and take on new roles.

5 · Frustration

Frustration is a common source of everyday stress. Frustration occurs when you want something you can't have or feel that things aren't the way you want them. Which seems to pretty much sum up life after a significant loss.

OTHER LISTS TO CHECK OUT:

Make Your Own List: What's Your Grief? (Your List of Losses), page 39

5 Realities of Acute Stress, page 74

6 Reasons Loss Creates Conflict with Others, page 131

---

what's your grief?

6

Things to Understand About Anger

Anger is a common and normal experience in grief, though this certainly doesn't make it a comfortable or easy one. For many, it is an overwhelming and even scary emotion. People are often taught that anger is an exclusively bad emotion that should be avoided, rather than learning to investigate anger and ameliorate their responses to it. But it is possible to change your relationship with anger. That doesn't mean the anger is going to disappear. But by approaching your anger from a place of awareness and without judgment, you can slowly shift the way you experience, perceive, and act on that anger. So let's take a minute to better understand what this emotion is all about.

1 ANGER IS OFTEN A FORM OF SELF-PROTECTION.

When you've been threatened or hurt, physically or emotionally, your evolutionary goal is to stop that pain. Anger can be a quick and easy way to feel like you're doing that. It's a way of saying, "I'm not going to take this," and that can make you feel strong in situations that are otherwise terrifying.

2 ANGER CAN BE A MEANS OF ASSERTING CONTROL.

Anger can feel like a more active emotion as compared to something like sadness or hopelessness. This can provide a sense of control—in other words, there can actually be an upside to anger.

3 ANGER LETS YOU SHOW SOMEONE THAT YOU'VE BEEN HURT.

If you're unhappy with how another person is acting or something they've done, expressing anger can be a quick way to get their attention. Often below this anger there is fear, sadness, disappointment, and a well of other emotions that can be tricky to unpack and talk about. But anger is often the protective emotion we show someone with the hope it will stop them doing whatever is bringing up those other emotions.

4 ANGER IS THE WAY SOME DEAL WITH GUILT, SHAME, AND REGRET.

You may find yourself feeling deeply angry at yourself. In grief, this may be because of regret, guilt and blame that you are still working through. Though it takes time and effort, practicing self-compassion and self-forgiveness can help to reduce this type of anger.

5 ANGER CAN BE BENEFICIAL. SERIOUSLY.

How anger serves you is all about what you do with it. If you find yourself throwing lamps and kicking dogs, that could be a serious problem. But if you can learn to notice anger, identify what triggered it, acknowledge the other emotions that arise with it, and allow it to serve as a catalyst for positive change, then we might classify your anger response as useful.

The benefits of anger echo what we have established as its purpose. Anger can serve as a catalyst for constructively:

- addressing negative circumstances and events in your life
- resolving differences
- identifying and fixing problems and maladaptive (or nonproductive behavioral) patterns in relationships
- protecting yourself from undesirable or threatening events, people, and circumstances
- helping you to find a route for action and control

6 HOWEVER, ANGER OBVIOUSLY HAS ITS DOWNSIDES.

Anger can negatively impact your physical and emotional well-being, your ability to participate in society, and your personal relationships. This is especially common if it is triggered frequently or bottled up, or if you don't have coping tools to manage it.

Chronic anger overworks your nervous system and inhibits your body's ability to deal with some of the more severe effects of adrenaline. Not to mention you may lash out and then regret anger-fueled behaviors. Side effects of anger include:

- **Poor physical health:** Those who experience anger regularly are at a higher risk of experiencing coronary artery disease, heart attack, high blood pressure, stiff arteries, and muscle tension. The risk of liver and kidney damage is also increased.

- **Poor emotional health:** This is most common for those who turn their anger inward, which is linked to higher depression and anxiety.
- **Isolation/poor social support:** Directing anger inward can lead to bitterness and passive-aggressiveness; anger expressed outwardly is just plain aggressive. Neither of these bodes well for relationships. If Oscar the Grouch didn't live in a world of Muppets, do you think he would have any friends?
- **Feeling out of control:** When you feel like you can't control anger triggers or deal with them properly, your feelings and emotions can start to feel chaotic and frantic.
- **Constant emotional arousal:** An inability to focus on anything but your inner state may leave you feeling out of touch with the outside world.

OTHER LISTS TO CHECK OUT:

8 Misconceptions About Blame, Anger, and Forgiveness, page 244
9 Tips for Communicating What You Do (and Don't) Need, page 233
4 Tips for Finding Calm in Your Grief Storm, page 203

6

Reasons Loss Creates Conflict with Others

Loss has a remarkable tendency to bring out the best and the worst in relationships. Maybe people you never imagined would be there for you come through in unexpected and amazing ways. Perhaps people you thought would be there for you ... weren't. Suddenly you may find yourself in the midst of conflict with people you'd never clashed with before. This can feel terrible, but it's not uncommon.

Reflecting on the common reasons why these tensions emerge is the first step to coping with them.

You're both grieving

Sometimes the loss you're going through is personal, but often it impacts your support system as well. If you and the other person are both grieving, you're both experiencing emotional strain and a bit of self-focus. It becomes hard to be empathetic to others' grief when you can barely manage your own. In some situations, the loss disrupts life-long dynamics. If your sister has always been your main emotional support person and you're both grieving the loss of your mother, she may now be unable to fulfill that role. This can create strain and friction.

(2)

You're grieving differently.

It's tempting to think that grieving alongside each other would mean you can always relate, but by now you probably understand why it isn't that simple. Grief looks different for everyone, even when you're grieving the same loss. Grief needs are different, grief styles are different, and such differences can create judgment and tension.

(3)

People want you to go back to normal.

When you've gone through a huge life change following a loss, others around you might be waiting for you to get back to normal or your old self. Meanwhile, you might feel like you've fundamentally changed and won't ever be the person you were before. This can be hard for you to communicate and even harder for another person to accept.

(4)

The loss caused people to take sides.

In cases of job loss, divorce, family estrangement, and many other situations characterized by division or blame, the ground is ripe for conflict. Sometimes these divides are obvious; other times they are subtle but lead to friction or distance that you didn't see coming.

(5)

Material possessions are involved.

This is particularly common after a death, but certainly not exclusive to death-related losses. Whenever there is child custody, money, sentimental possessions, a home, or other valuable possession, conflict can arise seemingly from out of nowhere. People who have always been agreeable and made decisions together can suddenly find themselves feuding, at a time when emotions are running high.

(6)

Roles and expectations have changed.

Losses can deeply impact your role with your family; your expectations of your friends and family members' roles might change. When it is unclear how roles are shifting, who will fill these changing roles, what people expect from one another, and how people are living up to those expectations, friction can quickly rise.

OTHER LISTS TO CHECK OUT:

9 Tips for Communicating What You Do (and Don't) Need, page 233

5 Questions to Ask Yourself Before Writing Someone Off, page 238

8 Misconceptions About Blame, Anger, and Forgiveness, page 244

What's Your Anti-Loneliness Wish List?

In the 1998 *Encyclopedia of Mental Health* researchers, Daniel Perlman and Letita Anne Peplau define loneliness as "the subjective psychological discomfort people experience when their network of social relationships is significantly deficient in either quality or quantity." In other words, loneliness occurs when a person's social relationships don't meet their interpersonal needs or desires. We want to note that the above definition says nothing about the state of being alone. Instead, that loneliness is a feeling of discomfort that arises when a person feels unfulfilled by their social relationships.

Individual loneliness is defined by what a person *wants* in relation to what they *have*. So whether a person has one hundred great family and friends, if they long for something or someone they don't have—such as an intimate partner or a friend they can open up to—they are liable to feel lonely.

Loss exacerbates loneliness for many reasons. Sometimes the person you've lost leaves a gaping hole in your life. Sometimes you find family and friends are distant after a loss. And sometimes your needs change in grief, for example, you may wish for someone who "gets you" or who is willing to sit and listen.

So here's what we want you to do:

- Get out a sheet of paper or a journal and spend a few minutes listing your interpersonal needs or desires.

- Ask yourself, "What are the qualities and characteristics I wish I had in my relationships?" Having an understanding of what makes you feel lonely should help to identify what's missing in your relationships and to potentially fill interpersonal needs in the future.

8

Risk Factors for Experiencing Isolation

A 2015 meta-analysis of nearly 35 years' worth of research on the impact of loneliness found that social isolation increased mortality rates by 29 percent, with the correlation highest in groups under 65 years old (Holt-Lunstad et al., 2015). A 2020 Cigna study of 4,885 individuals ages 10 to 97 found that younger generations were lonelier than older generations. Nearly eight in ten Gen Zers and seven in ten millennials identified as lonely, compared to half of baby boomers.

So when we raise the topic of loneliness and isolation, we do it not only because it is emotionally difficult, but because it has common and real health implications. Let's look at some of the biggest risk factors for social isolation after a loss, with the ultimate goal of helping you combat a bit of that grief-induced solitude.

1 YOU LIVE ALONE.

This sounds painfully obvious. But it is important that we're explicit about it, because if you're living alone after a loss, it is especially easy to hole up in a blanket fort with Netflix and Ben and Jerry's and refuse all human contact for weeks. Sometimes that might feel like the greatest gift you've ever been given. Alone time can be amazing. But alone time, which is a valuable time to self-reflect and recharge, is different from social isolation, which can become lonely and draining. Living solo means you have to be even more vigilant when it comes to keeping your social isolation in check.

2 YOU THINK THAT LONELINESS AND SOCIAL ISOLATION ARE THE SAME THING.

When you assess whether social isolation is impacting you, it is critical that you distinguish these two related, but different, things. Social isolation is the experience of having limited social interactions with other people. It is a behavioral experience. Loneliness, though defined in different ways, can be summarized as a feeling of distress caused by the perceived discrepancy between one's desired and actual levels of social relationships. That might mean having fewer relationships than you'd like, as well as not having the type or quality of relationships you desire. If you've ever been in a crowded room and felt alone, or had friends checking in on you but still felt lonely and disconnected, you know that loneliness and social isolation are not the same things.

3 YOUR LOSS WAS DISENFRANCHISED.

If you are experiencing a loss that isn't acknowledged or supported by society, friends, and family, it is no surprise you might feel yourself withdrawing and turning inward. If you feel like friends are minimizing what you are going through, rushing you, or not giving you space to talk about your loss, it can feel easier to pull away and isolate than fight for support and acknowledgment.

4   CONNECTING WITH OTHERS IS LOGISTICALLY DIFFICULT.

Some of the many possible factors that can make it challenging to connect with others are having a long-term illness, disabilities, limited access to transportation, living in a rural area, working from home, unemployment, or exposure to domestic or community violence. These don't mean you will experience social isolation, but they could increase your risk.

5   YOUR MOOD IS LOW AND YOUR FATIGUE LEVEL IS HIGH.

Connecting with other people can boost your mood and increase your energy. At the same time, it often requires energy to connect with others. You have to reply to texts. You have to plan a time and place to meet. You have to leave your cozy blanket fort. When you're struggling emotionally, these small barriers can feel like a full-on blockade. You might find your rational brain saying, *I know I would feel better if I met up with Jason for a walk*, while your fatigued emotional brain is busy saying, *That would take too much energy—stay in and watch four movies instead.*

6   YOU HAVEN'T EMBRACED HEALTHY-AVOIDANCE BREAKS.

Yes, avoidance can be a problem if it gets out of hand. But some healthy avoidance is not only okay, it's also useful. It is exhausting to be "working" on your grief all the time. In fact, you need to build in some distraction and balance, and connecting with others is a great way to do that. If you don't feel like you can ever take a break from your grief, you may cut yourself off from others.

7 YOU DON'T LIKE STRANGERS.

Who does? Okay, some people do. But everyone has different levels of comfort meeting new people and trying new things. If you don't have a strong support system (or at least not one nearby) and you don't like new people, this can be a major risk factor.

8 YOU KEEP TELLING YOURSELF THAT YOU'LL RECONNECT WITH PEOPLE WHEN YOU FEEL BETTER.

This is a common thought when grief is high or mood is low. You don't feel like seeing anyone, so you tell yourself that you'll wait and see people when you feel up to it. Problem is, that might be quite a while. And it turns out that seeing people might be the very thing that helps you to feel better.

OTHER LISTS TO CHECK OUT:

27 Things to Help You Feel Less Isolated, page 249

Make Your Own List: What's Your Anti-Loneliness Wish List?, page 134

3 To-Dos for Utilizing Your Support System, page 230

4

Things That Can Happen
When You Compare Losses

One thing we have noticed in our years of working with people experiencing losses of all types is the inclination to compare. People compare current losses to past loss: "This is the worst thing that has ever happened to me." And they compare their losses to other people's losses: "I was laid off, but it could be so much worse—my sister's house was just foreclosed and my neighbor's husband just died."

On the surface, such comparison might seem harmless. In fact, many people find comfort in the knowledge that suffering is a universal human experience.

(1)
You don't give yourself permission to grieve.

If you keep telling yourself that other people have it worse, you are minimizing your own experience. The reality is that we can always find someone whose situation seems worse than ours. Your loss doesn't need to be any worse than anyone else's for it to be valid, significant, or important. Someone's grief over losing a job, dream, relationship, person, or pet may seem bigger than yours—but no one's loss ceases to exist simply because it "could be worse." The existence of someone else's loss has no bearing on your own suffering. It's just something someone else is feeling.

There's enough room in the world for all the love and all the pain.

(2)
You cut yourself off from the support of others.

Experiencing a loss of any size can feel unexpectedly isolating. You may find yourself looking around and saying to yourself, "She could never understand, she's never had a loved one die" or "Even though he's also divorced, he won't be able to support me because his divorce was amicable." The tendency to compare is so common that grief expert Megan Devine aptly named it the "Grief Olympics." You may start judging others' losses as worse or better than yours, feeling like no one can support you because no one has had the exact same experience as you. Rather than thinking "No one will ever understand all of my grief, but some people can understand some aspects and provide some support," you may find yourself not opening up to anyone at all.

(3)
You beat yourself up for not coping as well as you have before.

We know from research that reminding yourself that you have survived past trials and tribulations can give you confidence in your ability to weather a current storm. That said, comparing how you managed a past loss to how you're coping with a current loss can sometimes backfire. Just like we talked about in the list of how new losses bring up old losses (see page 42), it is common to find yourself saying things like, "I handled things better when my father died and that was so much worse than losing my job. I shouldn't be such a wreck." But this isn't useful. The reality is that each loss is different and the way we manage each loss will be different.

(4)

You beat yourself up for not coping as well as others.

There are many wonderful ways for people to connect around loss experiences. From grief memoirs to podcasts, support groups to Instagram accounts, the world has slowly but surely created more creative outlets for people to express their grief. These are wonderful for reducing isolation and disconnection. Unfortunately, they make it harder to stave off comparisons. You might find yourself measuring your grief against the grief of others, chiding yourself for not grieving as "well" as someone else.

OTHER LISTS TO CHECK OUT:

9 Ways to Be Kind to Yourself While Grieving, page 200

4 Places to Look for Grief Support in Your Community, page 256

5 Items for Your Grief Not-to-Do List, page 58

5

Reasons It Can Feel Like Your Grief Has Been Forgotten

Though there are no universals when it comes to grief, there is one moment that many people can relate to after a loss. It is the moment when they realize their own life feels frozen in time while the world continues to turn. Perhaps a better description is one a woman once shared with us while trying to put words to her own grief. She said, "It's like my world is on fire, but I am the only one who can see it burning."

One of the unique challenges of loss is the feeling that you can think of almost nothing else, while others seem to have forgotten you're grieving. You're distracted at work, juggling secondary loss, and just trying to keep your head above water, but others are bustling around planning vacations, worrying about watercooler drama, or deciding which new sofa will look best in their living room. If you're feeling this way, it may be for one of the following reasons.

①

People have stopped checking in.

When you go through something difficult, friends and family are often great at checking in for the first couple of weeks. Maybe a month or so. Then the offers to help out and check-in texts slowly dwindle until it feels like no one remembers what you're going through.

②

People interpret you being out in the world with a smile as you "being fine."

Grief is an internal response to loss. Sometimes you'll make that experience externally visible. But many times you won't. Unfortunately, there will always be some people who see you looking outwardly okay as a sign that internally you're back to normal. The reality is often anything but.

③

Others are dealing with their own stuff.

Your loss is probably the most central thing happening in your life at the moment, just as your friends and family each have something central in their lives. Some have small and exciting things going on, while others have large and devastating things they're managing. Unfortunately, it's easy to forget what other people have going on when dealing with your own stresses. That isn't an excuse, it's simply a reminder that what can feel like thoughtlessness sometimes comes from another person being overwhelmed.

④

Your loss seems "less than."

Grief is not a competition, but your brain's tendency to compare can sometimes cause you to measure your loss against that of others. If you decide that others are going through something worse, you may minimize your own experience and feel as though it deserves less attention.

Your loss starts to feel unmentionable
(like the elephant in the room).

Family and friend groups tend to create a culture around how openly (or not openly) they discuss difficulties. You might find that people are not-so-subtly skirting subjects like that employer who let you go, or the party where they ran into your ex, or that wedding you missed because your mom was in hospice. Depending on your preference (and the person doing the skirting), you might be grateful for this avoidance. Alternately you might feel like this is an effort to ignore your loss and put it in the past.

OTHER LISTS TO CHECK OUT:

4 Things That Can Happen When You Compare Losses, page 139

9 Tips for Communicating What You Do (and Don't) Need, page 233

5 Ways to Get Comfortable with Grief, page 206

6

Ways Grief Can Change Your Priorities

We live a remarkable amount of our daily lives through habit. Though you may feel like you're making active and deliberate decisions all day long, according to researchers at Duke University, it turns out about 45 percent of the things you do each day are mindless routines (Neal, Wood, and Quinn, 2006).

This isn't a bad thing. Settling into the routine of life can be comfortable and reassuring and give your brain space to attend to other things.

But then, one day, loss tears through your world, taking your priorities along for the ride. Suddenly your job, the one that always seemed so important, doesn't anymore. Neighborhood gossip that used to be so juicy now seems vapid and empty. Some of the friends you've worked hard to stay connected with over the years just don't feel worth the time and energy.

What is it about grief that wrecks this kind of havoc on your values?

(1)

Loss disrupts your habits.

Loss can physically change your environment. It might change your routine. It might make previously easy tasks exponentially harder. This is significant, because the moment you switch your brain out of mindless-routine mode, you may start examining certain decisions that haven't felt conscious in a very long time. You might find yourself thinking, "Do I really want this Pop-Tart?" Or, "Wait a minute, do I even want this job?"

(2)
Loss clarifies what is important to you.

When you know what it's like to lose something important to you, be it a person, a job, your health, or your home, everything else starts to feel pretty inconsequential. You realize exactly how many things you would trade to get back whatever you lost, which can clarify the things you value most.

(3)
Grief forces you to protect your energy.

Grief is exhausting. It can emotionally and physically drain you until you feel like you're running on fumes. When you're in survival mode, you have no choice but to cut things that you don't have the bandwidth for. For example, spending your time at home with family suddenly seems more important than taking that extra shift at work.

(4)
Grief reminds you of your own mortality.

Whether it was the death of a loved one, a medical diagnosis, or an awareness of time passing, many losses serve as reminders that life is frightfully short. In an effort to take advantage of every moment, you might find yourself dislodging anything from your day that doesn't bring value.

(5)

Grief can make you more selfish.

Okay, selfish is harsh. How about self-focused? Sadness turns us inward and pain makes us self-protective (Bonanno, 2010). Couple that with the reminder that life is short, and suddenly the things you were doing strictly to please others seem like a waste of (precious) time.

(6)

Grief can make you more selfless.

On the other end of the spectrum, sometimes a heightened awareness of your mortality can push you to seek meaning. You start asking yourself big questions, like "What is my purpose here?" and "What will my legacy be?" You might find these existential questions moving you in new directions, inspiring you to sacrifice some of your own wants to help others.

OTHER LISTS TO CHECK OUT:

11 Questions to Ask Yourself as You Begin to Move Forward, page 276

7 Steps to Help You Live According to Your Values, page 167

5 Questions to Ask Yourself Before Writing Someone Off, page 238

3

Existential Questions Prompted by Loss

> *"Since all is empty, all is possible."*
>
> —NĀGĀRJUNA

People go through life believing certain rules are at play. "If I work hard, I'll be rewarded." "If I treat others well, they will treat me well in return." "If I obey my God, I will be protected from harm." "If I follow the rules of society, I'll be treated with fairness and equality." These are just examples, of course. Everyone lives with a different framework based on their unique background and experiences.

Though your framework for understanding the world may be built on a firm foundation, the structure itself is fragile. This is true for everyone because we can only build based on what we know. And throughout life, our experiences constantly introduce information that challenges, defies, and changes what we think, feel, and believe. So our worldviews are always under construction.

Loss can obviously challenge your existing ideas about life, death, mortality, the self, and others. And faced with truths that don't fit into your current understanding of existence, you may feel compelled to revisit some of life's biggest questions.

① What is the point?

This is a question that can be asked about many things. It is based on the assumption that your actions are working toward some end. Whether you realize it or not, so much of what you do on a day-to-day basis is done because on some level it serves a greater purpose. Like taking a road trip to a literal point on a map, you do all the driving, getting lost, and bickering with your copilot to eventually arrive at your destination. Without a destination, you're just wandering without a purpose or place to go. Loss sometimes feels like losing your destination. Suddenly, you have no sense of meaning and no direction. You're just aimlessly going through the motions, wondering what it all amounts to.

② What do I believe?

Changes to a person's belief system can cause considerable secondary loss. The loss experience may call into question a person's previously held beliefs about things like:

- Justice
- Fairness
- Equality
- Safety

- Loyalty
- Family
- Friendship
- Power

- Prejudice
- Trust
- Love
- God and religion

And the list goes on. It's important to note that questioning can sometimes lead to a deeper, more personal and nuanced belief system. Reconciling one's beliefs with contradictory life experiences can be a painful, humbling, and intimidating struggle, but it can often lead to growth and enlightenment.

(3) Am I spending my time well?

Asking yourself this question while grieving may seem like poor timing for a million different reasons. However, this is often precisely when people are most likely to ask it. As discussed on page 145, loss teaches you such profound lessons about yourself, your life, and the people surrounding you that it can drastically change your values and priorities. And when faced with big questions about life, death, and purpose, it's only natural to wonder if you're spending your limited time on earth well.

OTHER LISTS TO CHECK OUT:

6 Life Domains Impacted by Loss, page 48

6 Ways Grief Can Change Your Priorities, page 145

7 Steps to Help You Live According to Your Values, page 167

What's Your Identity?
(A Before-and-After List)

"When we mourn our losses we also mourn, for better or for worse, ourselves. As we were. As we are no longer. As we will one day not be at all."

–JOAN DIDION, *THE YEAR OF MAGICAL THINKING*

Identity is a funny thing. The ways we think of ourselves and the story we tell ourselves about who we are come together to create our identity. And yet we don't always have a conscious awareness of our identity. It often exists in the background, like the soundtrack of a film. We aren't fully aware of it until something changes.

When you experience a loss you are often focused on the tangible things you lose—the person, the house, the job, the relationship, etc. That's, of course, a huge part of grief. But as you now know, there are also secondary losses, and a loss or change in identity is a common one. Research has shown that the lack of "self-clarity" in grief that comes as a result of loss of identity is correlated with higher rates of depression and post-traumatic stress (Boelen, 2017).

So we want you to spend a little time thinking about your identity, looking at various aspects of it and considering how your identity has changed. Depending on your loss, you might see huge identity shifts or very small ones.

Relational Identity

This piece of your identity is based on your relationship with another person: sister, daughter, wife, friend, mother, caregiver, etc. Death-related losses can bring about a secondary loss or change related to your relational identity because someone like a sibling, parent, child, partner, or best friend has died.

Professional Identity

Phrases like "I am a teacher" or "I am a carpenter" or "I am a doctor" make clear that many of us consider our profession as a huge part of who we are. When someone loses a job, retires, or changes careers, they may experience loss around their professional identity. For example, someone who retires after forty years of teaching may struggle to conceptualize who they are and what gives their day structure and purpose now that they don't have lessons to plan or a classroom of students to lead.

Spiritual Identity

Whether a Christian, a Muslim, an atheist, a Buddhist, or someone who identifies as spiritual but not religious, you may have a spiritual identity that will grow, shift, shake, or disappear throughout your lifetime. As with tangible relationships, your abstract relationship with faith and spirituality may be impacted by life events. Loss is, of course, one such experience that can lead people in different directions, from a crisis of faith to an increased sense of spirituality and everywhere in between.

Financial Identity

Though people often don't think of finances as part of their identity, your ability to provide financially for yourself and your family might be an important component of your sense of self and your loss. Whether it is a constant state of financial struggle or pride in strong financial independence, you likely have an expectation about what your financial identity is, and your loss may have changed that.

Physical Identity

Physical identity defines how you are capable of physically existing in the world. In basic ways, like having the ability to work certain types of jobs, play with children, go for a walk or to the gym, and move free from pain, your physical self is fundamental to much of your daily life. Illness, injury, and aging can lead to a loss of physical identity that can sometimes be accompanied by a loss of self-worth.

Your Outlook

Though this can be hard to label, your outlook or perspective on the world can be deeply connected to your identity. As we've already shared, your worldview, outlook, and perspective can be shaken by trauma or loss. Whether it's being an optimist, believing that the world is a fair and just place, or thinking no one can be trusted, the lens through which you see the world has a deep impact on your identity. A significant loss can shake your assumptions about the world, leaving you feeling more negative, jaded, pessimistic, or unable to engage with other people or activities the way you used to. This can result in an identity change or loss that feels difficult to reconcile with who you used to be.

So here's what we want you to do:

- Grab a piece of paper and create a heading for each identity type you see on pages 152 and 153. You may wish to list them in columns (there are six total), it's up to you, but be sure to leave some space to write below or next to the heading.

- Under each identity type, take a few minutes to list your identity roles. As you write, think about what your identity was before the loss, what it is now, and, if applicable, what you hope it will be in the future.

Take a few minutes to reflect on what you've written. You may notice that you've experienced significant identity changes and wonder what to do about it. There is no easy answer. Like so many things in grief, trying to go back to how things were may not be possible. Part of regaining a sense of self after the loss is accepting that your identity is going to be different than it was before.

Also remember that different doesn't mean bad. As human beings, we often don't like change. We have ideas about how life is supposed to look and who we are supposed to be. When life doesn't pan out the way we expected, it can be easy to assume that no alternative will ever allow us to have a sense of well-being. Though there will always be a deep sense of grief around the people and things in life that we lose, it's possible that other things will bring purpose, joy, and contentment and will become new parts of your identity.

Finally, remember that identity is not black-and-white. It evolves and changes, and, in many cases, who you were before informs who you are now. In that way, your past is always echoing into the present and shaping the future. And as you lose one identity, it often opens up space for a new identity to grow.

5

Barriers to Coping with Grief

By now you hopefully have a deeper understanding of the thoughts, feelings, and behaviors that are part of your grief.

But there is the work to understand grief, and then there is the work to cope with the complex life that comes after loss. Though you might be desperate to navigate this complicated world, there are also things that will stand in the way. Following are some of those potential barriers.

(1)

You don't think that specific grief coping strategies will work for you.

Your personal narrative will have a significant impact on the coping you're willing to try. Telling yourself stories like "I'm not a good writer, so I can't journal" or "therapy isn't for me" or "I don't have time" will narrow the range of coping options that you'll entertain. It can be helpful to notice that little voice putting up a barrier between you and a coping tool; observe what it is saying, and then remind yourself that it might not be true and you can give things a try anyway.

You're worried moving forward means you're okay with the loss.

People often worry that starting the process of rebuilding after a loss somehow diminishes the significance of the loss or suggests that they're at peace with the loss having happened. We'll discuss this more on page 193, but suffice to say this couldn't be further from the truth.

The limbo of grief is more comfortable than the uncertainty of moving forward.

You know what life looked like before your loss. And as miserable and painful as your current reality might be, looking toward building an unknown and uncertain future can be terrifying. Between the energy required to take those steps, the decision-making that may be involved, and the fear of leaving the past behind, you may be tempted to stay in the painful present.

People start acting like your grief has an expiration date.

Though we know that there isn't an endpoint to grief, grieving people often receive subtle messages from family, friends, and society that their time to grieve is over days, weeks, or months after their loss. If the bereaved person believes these messages to any degree, they may question whether it's wrong to continue to carve out space and time for grief coping or whether they will still be welcome in grief support spaces like support groups and grief centers.

You believe your pain is what keeps you connected to the deceased.

If you've lost a loved one, it is likely that your love for them has become mixed up with pain and grief. You might feel that your suffering has become the expression of love lost, the way you honor your loved one, the one consistent link between life with them and life without them, and proof that their life left an indelible mark on others. Though there are so many other ways that you continue your connection to your loved one who died, an attachment to the anguish of grief as a part of your bond can get in the way of learning to cope with the pain.

OTHER LISTS TO CHECK OUT:

5 Little-Known Truths About Grief, page 19

4 Reasons to Love the Concept of Continuing Bonds, page 259

11 Questions to Ask Yourself as You Begin to Move Forward, page 276

PART THREE

Coping
with Grief

Now is the time to discuss how you forge your way from here. We know you're still standing amid the debris of your losses and your grief, but it should be clear by now that your losses are not things you leave behind. These experiences will be a part of whatever life you build as you move forward. Your losses will inform how you will reconstruct your world, and that is incredibly powerful. We promise.

The lists in this final section are designed to help you find ways to cope with grief and life after loss. They will push you to find things that calm and comfort you. They will encourage you to think about friends and family who can help. They will ask you to consider the world you want to rebuild for yourself now that the world you once knew is gone.

Living through loss may have changed your priorities. You may have found some relationships were strained, while others became stronger than ever. You may have survived experiences and emotions you never knew you could manage. You may no longer believe that the world is fair, safe, or just. You may have learned to accept that life after your loss will always be bittersweet.

The world you build from here will integrate each of those changes and many more. It will be informed by who you are now that you have lived through loss and found tools to cope. It will be a world in which meaning and hope live alongside loss.

One final note, as we begin our last section of lists: Though at times we will use words like *rebuild*, *progress*, and even *growth*, we realize how difficult it can be to believe these things are possible. So before you tell yourself you're not ready and shut the book, we want to acknowledge that most days, even the tiniest of lateral baby steps are all that is possible—and that's okay! Progress happens bit by bit in grief (which we'll discuss on page 162).

We won't force you to find acceptance, strength, gratitude, or happiness if you don't want to, now or ever. We will merely share coping ideas that could be helpful, and we'll discuss what we think can be possible after loss. If something doesn't resonate with you right now, we hope that instead of saying "no way, never," you'll say "maybe someday."

Dee

39

Signs That You're Making Progress

There are things in life that you can and should get over—for example, a cold or an argument with a good friend. Just imagine how much pain and negativity you'd carry around if you could never forget and move on. That said, it is a mistake to think that all painful experiences can and should be "gotten over."

Many people who've experienced serious hardship (for example, bereavement, illness or injury, addiction, mental health conditions) will tell you that healing isn't always about moving on. In fact, sometimes getting over or forgetting something isn't even desirable, like when a loved one dies.

We can see how the idea of grief and loss lasting forever may be frightening to those who think of grief as being only pain and sorrow. But grief doesn't condemn you to a life of darkness. Over time, as you find new ways to understand and cope with your loss, you will change your relationship with grief. What that relationship looks like is up to you to define. But grief should come to occupy a new—less dark and obtrusive—space in your life as you find ways to make peace with some of your pain,

Do you believe us?

It's okay if you don't. We get it. When something evolves as clumsily and slowly as grief does, it can be tough to visualize progress. On a day-to-day basis, you don't feel any better, and this perceived lack of improvement can be frustrating and defeating.

However, this nonprogress could just be a matter of perspective, especially if you're comparing yourself to your before or ideal self. In this instance, your before or ideal self may be based on the following things:

→ **The person you were before the loss:** Though you might know you will never be the same, it's hard not to idealize the person you were before you felt ravaged by the effects of grief. In your mind's eye, the person you were then may seem whole, unbroken, radiant, happy, and fulfilled. The way you see yourself now may pale in comparison to this "before" person.

→ **The person you believe you'll be when you feel better:** When you're feeling down, for whatever reason, it's common to think toward the future and imagine how much easier things will be when you're feeling better. But by looking forward to a nonexistent endpoint and staying focused on a mythical future you, you remain focused only on what you haven't accomplished.

If you truly want to gauge your progress in grief, we think you should compare yourself to your grief start point: where you were immediately following the loss or at the lowest point of your grief. This is the only way to see how far you've come. Even on some of your most difficult days, if you look all the way back to the beginning, you will likely notice that you've made steps forward.

And when we say steps, we literally mean steps—not strides. Grief is something that happens little by little and day by day. It is often six steps forward and three steps back. Healing from grief isn't the result of smoothly navigating a forward journey. Instead, it's what happens when you get up each day and decide to keep walking.

A while back, we asked our community, "How do you know when you're making progress in grief?" Here is their collective wisdom.

You know you're making progress in grief when . . .

1. When you're not on the floor crying . . .

2. When your stomach doesn't hurt quite as much . . .

3. When you're taking life day by day . . .

4. When you don't wake up with fire in your chest . . .

5. When you can get out of bed . . .

6. When you choose to take the next step . . .

7. When you've accepted the fact that it happened . . .

8. When you acknowledge you're experiencing grief . . .

9. When you accept grief isn't going anywhere . . .

10. When you let yourself feel the emotions of grief instead of pushing them down . . .

11. When you accept your emotions for what they are . . .

12. When you recognize you need help . . .

13. When you can tell your story without getting emotionally distressed . . .

14. When you can talk about it without shame . . .

15. When you can listen to certain songs without crying . . .

16. When you stop counting every week or month anniversary . . .

17. When you face places and things that remind you of your loss and don't have a panic attack . . .

18. When things that once triggered intense emotion bring you peace . . .

19. When the good days outnumber the bad days . . .

20. When your grief isn't breathing down your neck . . .

21. When grief doesn't even make you uncomfortable anymore . . .

22. When you stop obsessing over what could have or should have been and accept how it is . . .

23. When you find ways to process thoughts that used to lead you in circles . . .

24. When you start to believe you are capable of handling your grief . . .

25. When you choose healthy coping mechanisms instead of harmful ones . . .

26. When you're able to identify and plan ahead for difficult moments . . .

27. When you get out of the house . . .

28. When you make it to the next day, and then the next . . .

29. When you stop avoiding sad people . . .

30. When you want to be of service to others . . .

31. When you're in a good place to share with and support others . . .

32. When each day becomes more a celebration of life and less of a "what if" . . .

33. When guilt and regret fade away and create more space for gratitude and good memories . . .

34. When it makes you happy to talk about the past instead of making you cry . . .

35. When you start to see the color and light in the world again . . .

36. When you laugh and feel joy for the first time . . .

37. When you don't feel guilty for feeling happiness . . .

38. When you feel more peace . . .

39. When you're finally able to see the ways in which you've grown stronger.

OTHER LISTS TO CHECK OUT:

9 Ways to Be Kind to Yourself While Grieving, page 200

11 Questions to Ask Yourself as You Begin to Move Forward, page 276

5 Areas of Post-Loss Growth, page 278

7

Steps to Help You Live According to Your Values

"He who has a why to live for can bear with almost any how."

— FRIEDRICH NIETZSCHE

When you look back at your life before your loss, you probably see a place that made sense. You were moving along a familiar path, with familiar people, through familiar places. You'd probably sketched out a loose roadmap in your mind that guided you through twists and turns—school, jobs, friends, hobbies, partners, kids, life.

But then you experienced a significant loss. This can make you feel like you've been plopped down in the middle of unfamiliar territory. You vaguely recognize some people and places, but they're also different in a way that feels disorienting. They don't occupy the same space they used to in your life. All the familiar signposts are gone, and there is no trail of breadcrumbs to guide you back to the life you had before. Ultimately, *before* is gone. Loss has changed you; you're a new person navigating the unknown and unpredictable.

As the ancient Greek philosopher Heraclitus said, "No man ever steps in the same river twice, for it's not the same river and he's not the same man." Much of the work of living life after loss is learning this new world, discovering who you are within it, quietly making choices about where you are going, and creating a new path. Unfortunately, we can't give you a map to navigate this new world—no one can. But in the absence of a map, there is one tool you can use to help guide you: your values.

Your values are like a compass that helps clarify what matters most to you and points you in a direction that aligns with who you are and what you value at your core. When grieving, you are almost guaranteed to stumble and lose your way from time to time. But rest assured, as long as you're letting your values lead you, you're on the right path. If this all seems a little abstract or unattainable to you right now, we encourage you to read on. Using values to navigate life after loss is far more practical and common sense than it may seem.

1 LEARN WHAT VALUES ARE.

Stephen Hayes, the founder of acceptance and commitment therapy (one of our favorite types of therapy, for the record), describes values as "our chosen life directions" (Hayes, 2009).

Values are the guiding principles that help you decide what is important in life and how you want to behave. They help you decide how you want to treat yourself, treat others, and how you want to live in the world. Needless to say, they're pretty important. When people are living in a way that is out of sync with their values, they're often left feeling unfulfilled.

2   LEARN WHAT VALUES ARE NOT.

Values are not goals, and you won't "achieve" them. Also, your values are incredibly personal; no one else can define them for you. They are not something another person assigns to you the way that your boss might give you a work goal or your physician might give you a cholesterol-level goal.

We believe that values are far more helpful than goals in grief. Living with grief means experiencing setbacks, disappointments, changes, adjustments, etc. So focusing on goals alone can be frustrating, because grief can quickly get in the way of achieving them. Values, on the other hand, aren't focused on end points. Instead, they are focused on a direction.

3   UNDERSTAND WHY VALUES MATTER.

People who make decisions and choices that are consistent with their values, who spend their time living in accord with their values, tend to feel less anxiety and a greater sense of well-being (Kashdan, 2013). Some research has even shown that living in accordance with one's values is correlated with better physical health and longevity (Alimujiang, 2019).

4   EXPLORE WHERE VALUES COME FROM.

Your values have likely been shaped by your family, culture, spiritual beliefs, life experience, worldview, and even your personality. And though they may be shaped by things and people outside yourself, as we mentioned above, ultimately you determine your values. Also, they may evolve, change, and grow as you evolve, change, and grow.

5   CONSIDER WHY VALUES ARE ESPECIALLY IMPORTANT IN GRIEF.

After a loss, the world continues to turn—whether you like it or not. There will be everyday choices that you have to make, in the midst of a life that doesn't make sense anymore. In some cases, the people, hopes, and dreams that guided you before are gone. With so many other things lost, your values are the one thing you can always continue to lean on. People experiencing grief can feel grounded knowing that as long as they strive to live a life consistent with their values, they are headed in the right direction.

6   DO SOME "VALUES WORK."

Digging into values is a process that you can do formally or informally, on your own or with a therapist. It is both simple and complex. It involves clarifying the values that are important to you in different domains of your life. Refer to the box on the next page for examples. What values do you believe lead to a meaningful and purposeful life? How can those values guide the decisions and choices you're faced with?

7   REMEMBER THAT VALUES ARE NOT ABOUT HAPPINESS OR ELIMINATING PAIN.

Living in accordance with your values can give your life a greater sense of purpose and meaning, and that can, in some cases, ease pain and increase happiness. But that is not what values are for, and that is not always what happens. The reality of life, as you well know, is that we will not and cannot always feel happy. But living in the direction of your values can allow you to live with a greater sense of well-being, even when life is hard.

Examples of Common Values

You can begin exploring your values by considering which feel most important in each of the following areas of your life: family, relationships, friendship, work, leisure, personal growth, wellness, spirituality, community service.

Acceptance	Excitement	Order
Adventure	Flexibility	Perseverance
Authenticity	Forgiveness	Power
Balance	Freedom	Rationality
Beauty	Fun	Reciprocity
Care	Generosity	Respect
Challenge	Gratitude	Responsibility
Conformity	Honesty	Safety
Compassion	Humor	Self-care
Connection	Independence	Self-development
Contribution	Intimacy	Service
Courage	Justice	Skillfulness
Creativity	Kindness	Stability
Curiosity	Love	Trust
Equity	Mindfulness	Vulnerability

OTHER LISTS TO CHECK OUT:

6 Ways Grief Can Change Your Priorities, page 145

Make Your Own List: What's Your Identity? (A Before-and-After List), page 151

Make Your Own List: What's Your Reasons to Live List?, page 273

3

FAQs About Coping with Life After Loss

Coping is such a general and common term, people assume they know what it means without much consideration. And though they may get the gist of it, there's often a lack of specificity in their understanding, especially where grief is concerned. In this section, we talk a lot about coping. But first, we want to share our conceptualization of this term with you, so we're all on the same page.

①

What is coping?

From a psychological perspective, Wayne Weiten defines coping as "active efforts to master, reduce, or tolerate the demands created by stress" (Weiten, 2014).

Note Weiten makes no mention of the types of efforts used to master, reduce, or tolerate stress. Although the word *coping* often implies positive or effective attempts to feel better, people sometimes cope in ways detrimental to their mental, emotional, and physical health. This is what we call *negative coping*.

(2)

What is negative coping?

It's common to think of negative coping as specific behaviors that are typically considered bad: behaviors like excessive substance use, isolation, procrastination, etc. While these behaviors are certainly examples of negative coping, they don't provide a complete picture of the concept.

What makes a coping tool negative is how the behavior is used by the individual. Negative coping encompasses any behavior employed as a quick fix or a means to regularly avoid painful emotions or situations. Though these temporary distractions may reduce emotional pain in the short term, they provide very little actual healing. Negative coping is a bit like emotional aspirin; it numbs the pain temporarily, but once it wears off, the pain reappears. And because negative coping is almost always a form of avoidance, it can make things worse by preventing you from effectively processing your emotions and experiences, leading to a prolonged sense of anxiety and emotional pain. For a more detailed description of avoidance, head to pages 78 and 81.

(3)

How does WYG conceptualize constructive coping?

Our concept of coping is based on one of our favorite grief models, Margaret Stroebe and Henk Schut's dual process model of coping with bereavement (DPM), which describes the ways people cope with the loss of a close person. According to the DPM, coping happens in the context of everyday life and focuses on the following:

- **Loss-orientated stressors:** This refers to the processing of the loss itself and may involve yearning and rumination about the deceased, memories of the past, thoughts about the death, etc. A person copes with loss-orientated stressors on and off in an ongoing way over time.

- **Restoration-orientated stressors:** This refers to the attention one must give to adjusting to changes, secondary losses, and day-to-day life. These stressors might include taking on new roles, dealing with finances, and adjusting one's identity to accommodate a new reality.
- **Oscillation between the two:** An essential part of the DPM is *oscillation*, which refers to shifting back and forth between focusing on loss-oriented and restoration-oriented stressors, as well as what Stroebe and Schut call occasional "confrontation-avoidance." Under this model, a practical and adaptive part of grief is taking a break and seeking respite from it, as long as the avoidance isn't extreme or persistent.

Here's what we like about the DPM as it relates to coping with loss:

- It acknowledges that grief is an ongoing process that one has to learn to live with. There isn't an ultimate resolution, endpoint, or return to normal. Grief requires coping and adjusting on a day-to-day basis.
- It acknowledges the impact of secondary losses and secondary stressors, and that grieving people must spend almost as much time coping with these secondary stressors as they do dealing with the actual loss.
- It acknowledges that taking a break from grief can be adaptive and helpful for grieving people.

Following what we've learned from the DPM, it's necessary to find ways to cope with the thoughts, experiences, and feelings directly related to your loss. However, it's equally important to engage in coping that promotes adjustment and overall well-being. The rationale behind this is: the better you feel, the more strength you'll have for dealing with grief.

And even though you may not immediately realize it, there is a lot of overlap between loss-related coping and coping that promotes well-being. The coping you use to deal with loss can ultimately increase your sense of well-being, while much of the coping you use to maintain or increase your well-being can help you cope with loss.

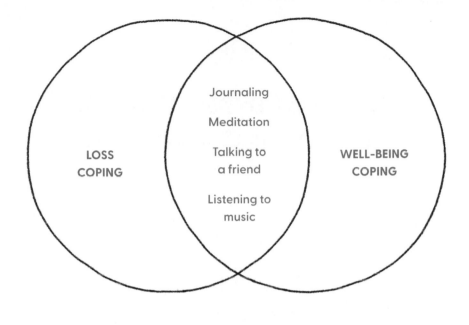

LOSS
COPING

Journaling

Meditation

Talking to
a friend

Listening to
music

WELL-BEING
COPING

OTHER LISTS TO CHECK OUT:

3 Things to Know About Avoidance, page 78
4 Questions to Ask Yourself About Your Coping Style, page 176
5 Building Blocks of Well-Being, page 182

4

Questions to Ask Yourself About Your Coping Style

The coping tools you use are unique to you, so we cannot tell you exactly how to cope. But the following questions can help you find tools and outlets that fit your specific strengths, personality, and preferences.

①

What's worked in the past?

On page 42, we suggested you start thinking about the coping tools that have helped get you through previous hardships. These tools have worked before, so there's good reason to believe they may work again.

②

What exactly are you coping with?

Remember when you made your list of losses on page 39? That list is a good starting point for understanding all the many things you have to cope with, which can also help you know which tools to use. Because coping with grief *always* requires dealing with a range of thoughts, emotions, and stressors, it's usually not enough to identify just one specific coping tool. Like real hammers and wrenches, you need the right one for the job.

(3)

What new types of coping would you consider?

If your existing coping skills don't feel adequate, know that this is normal. Many people find grief is such a new and overwhelming experience that they need an entirely different set of tools. It's also worth noting that you may feel cut off from coping outlets you used to find helpful because grief can cause you to feel disinterested in activities you once found fulfilling. Examples of this include feeling apathetic about creative outlets like journaling or art, or feeling disconnected from your support system. As you move through the final section of this book, we encourage you to consider trying new things to help you cope with your experiences.

(4)

What types of coping feel right for you?

Though we want you to have an open mind about coping, we don't want you to feel forced to engage with coping that goes totally against your grain. Unfortunately, it's not uncommon for grieving people to feel pressure to utilize coping outlets that make them uncomfortable. For example, our society tends to validate coping with grief by talking about it or "letting it out," so someone who would prefer more private or creative outlets may feel forced into a support group situation that feels counterproductive.

OTHER LISTS TO CHECK OUT:

Make Your Own List: What's Your Grief Style?, page 54

3 Types of Coping, page 178

5 Building Blocks of Well-Being, page 182

3

Types of Coping

Coping is in many ways an extension of our personalities. Traits such as whether you are introverted or extroverted, cautious or a risk-taker, analytical or emotional, a doer or a go-with-the-flow-er can influence the coping style that feels the most comfortable and appropriate.

Over the years, we've identified three different types of coping. This isn't a formal theory by any stretch. It's more like a framework that helps people identify the style that feels the most natural, constructive, and realistic given who they are and what they're facing. Of course, grieving people often have to try many different coping outlets before finding the ones that work. But having an awareness of your personal preferences, time, and resources from the outset can help make this search a little less rocky.

Also, these three types are not categorical, meaning you don't have to box yourself into just one. Your preferences and personality traits exist on a continuum, and so does your coping.

① Emotional Coping

Grief can make you feel all sorts of emotions—big and small, familiar and unfamiliar. Experiencing, processing, and expressing these emotions can help you understand and integrate them in a meaningful and healthy way. Additionally, becoming comfortable with these difficult emotions can help you be more sympathetic toward others. Some people are very comfortable within this emotional realm, and in challenging situations, they tend to focus on feeling and expressing their emotions.

Examples:

- Looking at old photos and having a good cry
- Talking to a friend, family member, therapist, or support group
- Reading grief memoirs to connect with the emotional experiences of others

② Creative Coping

People can express their creative selves in many ways, such as photography, journaling, art therapy, scrapbooking, and music. The emotions of grief are difficult to understand and share, and for some people, creative outlets can make it easier to face difficult emotions in nontraditional ways.

You may think if you don't create, you aren't creative. But in reality, you can connect with your creative side by appreciating the artistic expression of others. Viewing art and movies, reading books, or listening to music can connect you with the creator's experience and help you reflect on your own experience.

Examples:

- Writing your grief story
- Writing, listening to, or sharing songs that resonate with your emotions

- Taking photographs that capture an aspect of your loss or grief
- Creating a scrapbook or memory book to memorialize a person, place, or time in your life

③
Rational Coping

Some people have a more hands-on and rational approach in times of loss and hardship. For them, knowing, understanding, intellectualizing, learning, and doing brings a sense of security and comfort.

People who relate to this grief style may want to understand their experience by learning more about grief, mental health, and concrete coping tools. They may find comfort in handling practicalities, such as sorting belongings or preparing for anniversaries and special days. These tasks can provide order and stability to people who cope this way.

Examples:

- Learning about grief models and theories (see page 34)
- Putting together a slideshow honoring a deceased loved one
- Organizing a fundraiser in support of a cause connected to your loss

---

Now that you've read through the coping types, ask yourself the following questions:

⟶ When you think about the types of coping you've used in the past, do you notice any commonalities or themes among them?

⟶ Do you tend toward dealing in ways that are emotion focused, creative, or rational and pragmatic?

→ Do you notice that you're channeling your grief into certain creative outlets?

→ Do you feel better after expressing your emotions?

→ Are you drawn toward introspection, analyzing, or learning about grief?

OTHER LISTS TO CHECK OUT:

3 FAQs About Coping with Life After Loss, page 172

4 Questions to Ask Yourself About Your Coping Style, page 176

Make Your Own List: What's in Your Coping Bucket?, page 185

5

Building Blocks
of Well-Being

Just like the experience of happiness, well-being is subjective and can mean different things to different people. Some ways one might describe well-being after loss include words like feeling okay, good, satisfied, balanced, or at peace. Or one might feel they have purpose and meaning, healthy relationships, and a sense of pride in personal accomplishments. Those who are grieving someone or something they love might also say that being able to appreciate the present while remaining connected to the past is an essential part of their sense of well-being.

What we just described might sounds far off to you. We promise, no one is expecting you to feel great tomorrow. However, by understanding the elements that contribute to well-being, you can choose coping that increases your sense of well-being. And rest assured, however unattainable an overall sense of well-being may seem, coping that promotes well-being is very accessible.

We'll look at coping that encourages well-being using the framework of positive psychology's well-being theory. This theory is outlined in the 2011 book *Flourish* by Martin Seligman. It is a detailed theory, but for our purposes we want to focus on what Segliman defines as the five building blocks of well-being. Each person will value these building blocks differently. But generally speaking, choosing to enhance or engage with any of these areas can foster a sense of well-being.

1 · Positive Emotions

First, we need to note that experiencing positive emotions is not the same as being happy. We are not trying to rush you away from your grief toward a more positive mental state. What we are talking about here is experiencing occasional moments of positive emotions alongside your grief.

Ask yourself, what are the little things that tend to make me smile or feel good, even temporarily? Maybe it's looking at pictures of your grandkids, baking, playing with your dog, or watching your favorite guilty pleasure reality TV. In the grand scheme of things, these activities won't heal your grief, but they can provide a brief respite from your suffering and slowly help to increase your sense of well-being.

2 · Engagement

Engagement happens when you are participating in activities that fully absorb you in the present moment, grabbing your whole focus and creating the sense that time is flying by. Things a person might consider engaging in include sports, music, cooking, photography, woodworking, reading, and jigsaw puzzles.

3 · Relationships

People are social animals. Regardless of whether you identify as an introvert or extrovert, you need *some* social connection. For that reason, we encourage you to nurture any positive relationships you have. And, if you feel your social support is lacking, we'll discuss ways to reach out and connect with others on page 249.

4 · Meaning

Meaning speaks to a person's purpose in life. To a degree, your purpose probably coincides with your values. As we discussed in the previous section, grief can change a person's sense of meaning, in good ways and bad. On the positive end, grief can provide a person with a new purpose in life. For example, after a loss, many people find themselves drawn to volunteering or advocacy work on issues related to their loss.

5 · Accomplishments

Personal achievements can give you a sense of satisfaction and pride. These don't have to coincide with outward accolades, awards, or titles, although they can. Anything that gives you a feeling of gratification for having succeeded, survived, or finished can be considered an accomplishment. Your accomplishments—and what you would *like* to accomplish— are specific to you. However, we think any progress you've made in grief is an accomplishment.

OTHER LISTS TO CHECK OUT:

7 Steps to Help You Live According to Your Values, page 167

3 FAQs About Coping with Life After Loss, page 172

Make Your Own List: What's in Your Coping Bucket?, page 185

What's in Your Coping Bucket?

Most people are familiar with the idea of a bucket list, which is a collection of hopes, dreams, and goals a person wants to accomplish in their lifetime. For this list, we're going to adapt this concept a little.

By our definition, a "coping bucket list" is a collection of coping strategies that a person (1) has tried and wants to do more of, or (2) would like to try. This list should include ideas for coping directly with grief as well as ideas for enhancing well-being.

Here are a few additional considerations:

- Your list should reflect your individual preferences, values, and overall hopes for the future. So, for example, if you prefer to grieve privately, you don't have to include something like "attend a support gathering" on your list.

- Keep in mind that grief changes over time. If you believe that some day you might be interested in taking an online course on grief, but you're not up to it right now, still include it.

So here's what we want you to do:

- Get out a sheet of paper or your journal and start your coping bucket list. This list is evolving and ever-changing, so you don't have to finish it right now.

- When you've finished adding everything you can think of today, set your list aside in a safe place.

- Pull your coping bucket list out on days when you need extra help coping or when you want to add or remove coping ideas. If you need a little inspiration, we've included some coping ideas on the following page.

GET PHYSICAL

Dance

Exercise

Play a sport

Ride a bike

Hike

Walk

Run

Stretch

Skateboard

Surf

Swim

Move any way your body wants to move!

GET OUT

Go to a concert

Go to a comedy show

Go to the movies

Go to the theater

Go out to eat

Go to a sporting event

Go to a coffee shop

Go to the library

Walk around your neighborhood

Plan a fun day with your kids, your partner, or a friend

Go shopping

Take a vacation

GET EMOTIONAL

Cry

Yell

Vent

Talk about the past or deceased loved ones

Participate in remembrance activities

Look at old photos

Start a gratitude journal

Express love

Express anger

Write a letter to someone who let you down

Seek forgiveness

Grant forgiveness

GET WELL (BEING)

Meditate

Cook

Bake

Watch television

Watch movies

Watch grief-themed
television or movies

Listen to podcasts

Watch funny videos

Play

Take a break from social media

Take a warm bath

Unplug from work

Laugh at yourself

Schedule your doctor's
appointments

Attend religious services

Pray

Clean

Cut back on alcohol

Try a new hobby

Eat something delicious

Take a nap

Go for a drive

Snuggle

Sing

Get organized

GET CONNECTED

Participate in virtual
support gatherings

Participate in in-person
support gatherings

Follow grief pages on social media

Post grief-related content
on social media

Talk to a friend or family member

Share stories

Send a card to someone you think
would appreciate it

Check on someone who's going
through a difficult time

Perform a random act of kindness

Say you're sorry

Say thank you

Plan a party

Call a friend

Get a meal with a friend

GET CREATIVE

Do creative writing
Write poetry
Take photographs
Draw or doodle
Paint
Sculpt something
Write music

Listen to music
Play an instrument
Quilt or sew
Do a craft
Scrapbook
Do woodworking

GET INFORMED

Read self-help books
Read grief websites
Read academic books or articles
Learn about grief
Learn about issues related to your loss

Take online courses
Participate in grief webinars
Go back to school
Take a class

GET INVOLVED

Volunteer
Advocacy
Coach
Teach

Start an advocacy group
Start a nonprofit
Give to charity
Run a charity drive

GET INSIGHT

Journal
Write your story
Seek individual therapy
Seek group therapy
Seek couple's or family therapy

Talk to a friend about
your experiences
Self-reflect
Read memoirs

what's your grief?

50

Six-Word Stories About Grief

Legend has it, while out to lunch with fellow writers the author Ernest Hemingway bet his friends he could write a short story in just six words. His companions had their doubts and wagered ten dollars each to put Hemingway to the test. As the tale goes, Hemingway wrote the following story:

"For sale. Baby shoes. Never worn."

Although the validity of this anecdote is contested, there's absolutely no question this is a darn fine short story. Like all stories, it has the basics—a beginning, middle, and end—as well as all the things that make a story great: emotion, detail, and interest. The tale of Hemingway's "baby shoes" story continues to interest literary fans to this day, and six-word stories (sometimes classified as short short stories or flash fiction) can be found everywhere from tweets and blogs to galleries and anthologies.

We like six-word stories, especially when talking about feelings and emotions. Discussing feelings often makes people nervous and uncomfortable, so many people simply don't do it. But six-word stories are perfect little bite-sized emotional expressions. Though you may think that six words sounds limiting, in fact it can feel strangely freeing. It relieves the pressure of writing a perfect and precise story or explanation.

The key to the six-word story is finding the perfect words to communicate your point. You might strive for a beginning, a middle, and an end; however, we value substance over form, and whatever six words you want to string together is A-OK with us.

In 2016 we created a minisite called Grief in Six Words where people can share their stories and expressions about grief. We have received thousands over the years and share fifty here.

1. This pain was not my choice.—Shea

2. Trouble finding life's meaning without you.—Barry

3. My friends are fictional characters. Alone.—Umma

4. Addiction. Homeless. Are you still alive?—Chris

5. My son died inside of me.—Kate

6. Six words can't express my regrets—Holly

7. I wonder if I did enough.—Martinezes

8. Brother, I didn't know you existed.—Cora

9. Unexpected love in an unwanted pregnancy—Elle

10. Inside my delusion, you seemed happy.—JH

11. Heard a phone ring, wasn't you.—Renee

12. Ashamed I complained about life before.—Dawn

13. Get sober; I miss us laughing—Robin

14. My skin is screaming for touch—Andrea

15. I aspire to bring you back—Laura

16. Incurable disease closed many possible futures.—Dan

17. I did deeply love my house.—Laurel

18. Learning to talk to you differently.—Samara

19. Absolute isolation, living but not breathing.—Luna

20. No baby. Still no baby. Still.—DJ

21. Anorexia took everything including your heart.—Jodie

22. She was four, cancer doesn't care.—Emily

23. Anticipatory. When will it happen: Heroin.—RZ

24. Childless but changed by you forever.—Lisa

25. Wishing to play with your curls.—Jess

26. World, please stop while I grieve.—Nancy

27. Months ago my name was Mommy.—Audrey

28. Death is coming sooner than expected—Mike

29. Where is the sign you promised?—Anthony

30. His heartbeat: music to my ears—Renee

31. Did the devil make you jump?—Jane

32. Life keeps moving, I am frozen.—Anna

33. You wrecked my heart so beautifully.—Bethany

34. Missing the joy you made me feel.—Kathleen

35. I felt claimed without being wanted.—Natalie

36. Still can't find the light switch.—April

37. I was not back in time.—Dak

38. No no no no no no.—Liz

39. Our world spins without its sun.—Becky

40. What if the cancer comes back?—Hanna

41. There is no silver lining, anywhere.—Jules

42. Grief precedes death like an avalanche.—Peggy

43. Family memories buried with you, Grandma.—Amber

44. I feel like a rudderless ship.—Nadine

45. You assume there is a tomorrow.—Melissa

46. Grief only exists where love lived.—Amy

47. "We'll speak later!" We didn't.—Sophia

48. Year 2: I kept your stuff.—Alex

49. I have greatly harmed another. Help.—Lois

50. It won't always be this way.—Dawn

OTHER LISTS TO CHECK OUT:

64 Things We Wish We'd Known About Loss, page 23

3 Types of Coping, page 178

16 Questions to Help You Understand Your Grief Story, page 282

4

Things You Can Do to Cope with Conflicting Emotions

When we discussed living with mixed-up emotions after loss (see page 70), we explained that grief often requires flexibility to accept feeling two (or more) seeming conflicting things at the same time. We slipped it in there, casually, like it was no big deal. But having that flexibility is a big deal—a very big deal, in fact, because it opens up a hugely import-ant new way to understand grief.

That said, achieving this flexibility can be easier said than done. It doesn't come naturally to most and requires some learning (and un-learning) of how you experience thoughts and feelings. You see, the mind wants to ease feelings of conflict or ambivalence by letting one emotion win. And until you get used to allowing more than one to exist, you'll often have to remind yourself that your feelings aren't at war.

Here are a few ways to practice having greater emotional flexibility

① Remind yourself that your capacity for emotions is not finite.

The first step to getting comfortable with conflicting emotions is realizing that emotions can coexist fully, never taking away from one another. And there is always more space for new emotions. When parents get pregnant with a second child, no one says, "Oh, isn't that a shame, they're going to have to take some of their love away from their son to give it to this new baby." Instead, people intuitively know that the parents' capacity to love will grow to envelop that child.

② Learn about dialectical thinking.

Dialectical thinking is when one can hold two seemingly contradictory thoughts or feelings at the same time. As we've discussed, this is not easy. As humans, we like things to be in nice, neat, tidy boxes: Good or bad. Happy or sad. Right or wrong. The older you get, the more moments you encounter that challenge that wish. The power of dialectical thinking is that it often opens a new space for something more nuanced to emerge. When you acknowledge that both things can be true, it allows you to cope in new ways.

③ Cut out either/or and always/never thinking.

Examples of these kinds of thinking include:

- Life didn't turn out the way I expected so I will never be happy again.
- My friends are rushing me in my grief; they are terrible friends.
- No one can help me because no one understands my grief.
- I tried a support group once and I didn't like it, so therapy and groups aren't for me.

(4) Adopt both/and/sometimes thinking.

Examples of both/and/sometimes thinking include:

- I will never be happy in the way I imagined, and I am still capable of happiness.
- My friends are not providing me the grief support I need right now, but they have been good friends in the past and may be capable of being good friends again.
- No one understands my grief, but people in my life may still be able to help me in other ways.
- I tried a support group that I did not like. It wasn't right for me, but another group or therapist might be a better fit.
- I'm devastated by this loss, and I am relieved that my loved one is no longer suffering.
- I would give anything to have my loved one back, and I have grown as a result of this loss.
- I've been destroyed by what I lost, and I am grateful for what I still have.

In each of these examples, the initial thought is not false or replaced. It is not diminished. Rather, multiple thoughts are fully true and exist alongside one another. With both/and/sometimes thinking, there is often new flexibility or space that emerges.

OTHER LISTS TO CHECK OUT:

4 Facts to Remember When Life Doesn't Turn Out
the Way You Planned, page 270

Make Your Own List: What Are Your Grief Emotions?, page 68

6 Mixed-Up Emotions You May Feel in Loss, page 70

7

Steps to Help You Cope When You Don't Feel Like Coping

Picture it: it's been a long week, you're tired, the weather's not great, and it is utterly impossible to imagine anything as enjoyable as changing into your pajamas, ordering a pizza, opening a bottle of wine, and settling in for some quality couch time. Yes, you have plans to go to a book club with friends and you have been feeling lonely and isolated for weeks now. But you just don't have the energy tonight. It's okay to cancel just this once, right? You're grieving, after all. And Netflix and a comfy blanket is self-care, right? No one really gets what you're going through anyway. When you feel a little better in a couple of weeks you can reschedule.

We engage in these mental gymnastics all the time, and we bet you do too. Coping when you don't feel like coping can feel like an insurmountable task. Sometimes you know something would be good for you, but you still can't bring yourself to do it. There can be a massive chasm between what you know you should do to take care of yourself and what you actually do. The tips below aren't intended to launch you all the way across that chasm. But they can help you start to inch your way closer. And they're loosely inspired by an evidence-based therapy for coping with depression called behavioral activation (Lewinsohn et al., 2011). Though grief isn't the same as depression, we've seen this approach benefit people grieving time and again.

① Make a list of the things you've stopped doing since your loss that you used to love and find fulfilling.

Big things, small things, any things. Remember that doing things you used to enjoy, that helped you cope in the past, or that you find meaningful is coping with grief. Remember what we said about well-being, coping, and values? (If not, see pages 167, 172, and 182.) Though people often think coping with grief has to look like support groups, therapists, and writing about your feelings, reconnecting with your passions (or even reconnecting with a friend, going for an evening walk, playing basketball, or getting your nails done) can absolutely help you cope with life after loss.

② Next to each one, write down the reason(s) you've stopped doing that thing.

Some common reasons are: you don't feel up for it, it requires too much effort, it reminds you of the past (in a bad way), you don't have the time, you don't have the money, it seems less fun than before.

③ Stop saying, "As soon as I feel better, I'll start doing X again," and instead say, "Doing X again might be what helps me feel better."

We know, this sounds like some sort of cheesy self-help mumbo jumbo, but there is real research supporting this shift in thinking.

(4)

Ask yourself: what does a typical day currently look like?

Literally, write down your hour-to-hour schedule. Ask yourself how many activities are there in your schedule that help you (1) take care of yourself, (2) directly cope with your grief, and (3) feel positive feelings? What used to be a part of your schedule that you've now stopped doing?

(5)

Make a plan to do stuff.

To start, select at least two activities you will reintroduce this week. Now, literally schedule them at specific times like any other appointment. If you need to adjust your schedule—to make sure you get up early enough, or ensure you leave work on time—do so. If you think you might need a little external push, enlist a friend or family member to keep you accountable.

(6)

Remember, you often won't want to do these things, and yet you can still do these things.

Remember when you were a kid and you *really* didn't want to do something and an adult said, "Tough luck, you're doing it anyway," and you did? As an adult, sometimes you need be the one who tells yourself, "Tough luck, you're doing it anyway." So when you think that you don't want to go on that walk you scheduled, notice the thought, label it as a thought, and then say to yourself, "I'm having the thought that I really don't want to go on this walk and should skip it. But tough luck, I'm taking the walk anyway, because I said I would and I know it will be good for me."

(7)

Anticipate your excuses and rationalizations, and be ready with a response.

Once you've started to notice that little voice in your brain that tries to talk you out of coping, you'll start to notice some common refrains. "You can go next week instead." "You've had a terrible week, you deserve to sulk." "No one understands you anyway, so why bother going?" Start writing down the ones that come up the most often. For each one, write down at least one response to counteract that thought. This is not about invalidating the thought or proving yourself wrong. Rather, it is about reminding yourself of your values and the reasons for coping even when it's difficult.

OTHER LISTS TO CHECK OUT:

Make Your Own List: What's In Your Coping Bucket?, page 185

5 Barriers to Coping with Grief, page 155

4 Questions to Ask Yourself About Your Coping Style, page 176

9

Ways to Be Kind to Yourself While Grieving

Imagine you're talking to a close friend who is grieving, and she tells you she's frustrated because she doesn't think she's coping well. She wonders whether she is strong enough to handle her grief. She regularly compares herself to others in her grief support group, whom she believes are coping better than she is.

From an outsider's perspective, you've noticed that she's made many active efforts to cope, and you've seen her push herself to take small but difficult steps forward.

Now, assuming this friend appreciates feedback, what would you say to her? Would you say something compassionate, supportive, and encouraging?

Of course you would.

Now think about a time when you were the frustrated and self-critical grieving person. Even if the content of your criticism was different, the self-reproach was the same. What, at that time, did you say to yourself? Did you show yourself the same support and encouragement that you gave to your hypothetical friend above? If the answer to this question is, "No, I was not kind to myself," you are definitely not alone.

It's puzzling, isn't it? Why do we respond to our friends with understanding, patience, and compassion but react to ourselves as though we're hard-nosed football coaches running drills before the big game?

"You call that grieving? At this rate, you'll never feel better! Now take a lap!"

If you think about it, most of us are taught to be kind to others at a very early age, but lessons about being kind to oneself are far less overt. This is an unfortunate reality because self-compassion has been linked to increased resilience and well-being and lower levels of depression, anxiety, and stress. (Smeets et al., 2014).

Self-kindness and compassion can go a long way during times of loss, stress, and hardship. When you're struggling at a very fundamental level, the last thing you need is for your inner voice to question your every thought and action. And when you've finally worked up the courage to look at some of your most feared thoughts and emotions, as this book has challenged you to do, you need a cheerleader in your corner, not a critic.

We know words like *self-kindness* and *self-compassion* can feel fluffy. To clarify, we're not asking you to start doing daily affirmations if that's not your thing (but if it is, have at it!). All we're asking is for you to think practically about how you can be a little nicer to yourself, both in your thoughts and actions. Here are nine suggestions to get you started.

1. REMEMBER—YOU HAVE THE RIGHT TO FEEL HOW YOU FEEL ABOUT YOUR LOSSES.

2 REMIND YOURSELF THAT THERE IS NO ONE WAY THAT GRIEF *SHOULD* BE AND NO SINGLE WAY THAT YOU *SHOULD* COPE.

3 REVIEW OUR DISCUSSION ON SHAME AND SELF-STIGMA ON PAGE 104.

4 ENGAGE WITH OTHERS IN BIG OR SMALL WAYS.

5 ALLOW YOUR EMOTIONS TO EBB AND FLOW.

6 TAKE LIFE ONE MINUTE, HOUR, AND DAY AT A TIME.

7 MEASURE YOUR PROGRESS BASED ON WHERE YOU STARTED WHEN YOUR GRIEF BEGAN.

8 DON'T BE ASHAMED OR EMBARRASSED TO ASK FOR OR ACCEPT HELP.

9 ALLOW YOURSELF TO TAKE BREAKS FROM YOUR GRIEF.

OTHER LISTS TO CHECK OUT:

---

what's your grief?

4

Tips for Finding Calm in Your Grief Storm

Maybe we should have warned you that when we asked you to explore your grief, we were really asking you to dive into the pain and keep swimming.

We were asking you to tolerate it, sit with it, and even embrace it. That is a tall order when you're feeling low. Maybe we didn't spell this out explicitly sooner because we knew that you were probably feeling pretty bad when you first cracked open this book. If we'd started with that, you might not have stayed with us. Here are a few tips for taking care of yourself and calming down when grief feels tough.

(1)

Know your grounding exercises.

When your brain gets overwhelmed by thoughts and feelings, grounding into your body and the world around you can help you calm down. *Grounding* is just a therapy-type word that means shifting your focus to connect with the present moment. There are many grounding exercises out there, so find those that are best for you. Some that might help are:

- **Breathing exercises.** A good one to start with is a box breath: inhaling for a count of 4, holding it for 4, exhaling for 4, holding for 4, and continuing this pattern.

- **Engage your senses.** A great technique is the 5-4-3-2-1. Look around and identify 5 things you can see, 4 things you can touch, 3 things you can hear, 2 things you can smell, and 1 thing you can taste.
- **Mindfully make yourself a warm drink.** This may sound basic or silly but taking a step away from what you are doing to focus on carefully making yourself a warm, comforting cup of tea, coffee, or hot chocolate can bring you back into the present moment. Notice the smell of the coffee or tea. Pay close attention to the size, shape, and feel of your mug. Keep your awareness on the warmth and flavor of the drink as you lift you mug and take a sip.

(2)
Go at your own pace.

Learning to cope with life after loss is a marathon, not a sprint. It isn't something you will work really hard at, master, and move on. It is a slow evolution that happens over time through learning, processing, coping, and growing. It is exhausting and it is important to remember to go slow, take breaks, and engage in that healthy avoidance we told you about from the dual process model (see page 34).

(3)
Plan self-care after spending time with difficult emotions.

If you know in advance that you're going to spend time facing and processing challenging emotions, such as in a therapy session, with a friend, in your journal, or through your artistic expression, plan some downtime after. Give yourself the space to decompress, connect with things you love, and recharge with whatever form of self-care feels good to you.

(4)

Show yourself that kindness and self-compassion we've been talking about.

When your emotions are high, when coping is hard, when you can't seem to calm yourself down, you may find yourself thinking you should be doing a better job. You might even work yourself up *more* by beating yourself up for not being able to calm down! This is a moment when showing yourself self-compassion is critical. We know it isn't easy (and if you need some help being gentle with yourself, turn back to page 200).

5

Ways to Get Comfortable with Grief

> *"There's no 'should' or 'should not' when it comes to having feelings. They're part of who we are and their origins are beyond our control. When we can believe that, we may find it easier to make constructive choices about what to do with those feelings."*
>
> —FRED ROGERS (AKA MISTER ROGERS)

We are a culture that values mastery. We value control over situations, problem solving, and being solutions focused. Don't get us started on our love of labels, systems, and standard operating procedures.

But as the boxer Mike Tyson once said, "Everyone has a plan until they get punched in the mouth." Major losses are antithetical to the idea of mastery that is drilled into many of us from childhood. They are often unplanned and unexpected. Our productivity and efficiency implode. Circumstances cannot be controlled. The emotional upheaval that ensues doesn't fit into any neat, tidy system.

Unfortunately, our culture rarely flexes to accommodate the needs of grief. People sing the praises of those who are "strong" and "brave" in times of crisis. In the US there is an accepted standard of three days of bereavement leave, a pat on the back, and the expectation to get back to work. Society gives you a grief gold star if you never skipped a beat on your volunteering and kids' activities during your divorce.

Even if you're frustrated with those messages, you've probably also internalized some of them. From childhood, we hear messages like: *Chin up. No tears. Stay busy. Happy is good. Sad is bad. Angry is really bad. Don't focus on the problem, focus on the solution.* Getting comfortable with grief means getting comfortable pushing back on those external expectations and that voice in your head telling you how you should grieve and, instead, accepting your grief as it comes.

(1)

Stop judging your grief.

Grief is a normal and natural response to loss. It is not something to be cured, solved, or fixed. Whatever your preconceived beliefs about what you are allowed to grieve, when you can grieve, and what feelings you should (or should not) be having, work to let them go while also accepting your grief for what it *is*.

(2)

Stop worrying about others' reactions to your grief.

This can take many shapes. You might find yourself worrying that your grief is too much or not enough. You may be overly concerned about whether others understand your grief or not. You could find yourself concerned about whether your grief is making them uncomfortable. The list goes on. Take a deep breath, let it out, and remember that your job is to accept and tend to your grief emotions. It is not to worry about how others respond to your grief.

(3)

Stop avoiding your feelings.

A little bit of healthy avoidance is a nice break; chronic avoidance is a problem. If you think your tendency to avoid is preventing you from coping with grief or impacting your day-to-day life, remind yourself that you can take steps to reduce avoidance and start facing your loss. Gauge whether you're engaging in avoidance by considering these questions.

- Are you staying away from certain people that might talk about your loss or be a reminder of your loss?
- Are you avoiding places or even objects that bring up memories of your loss?
- Are you drinking more or using other substances to numb or avoid thinking about your loss?
- Are you focusing all of your free time and attention into work, taking care of others, or a hobby to avoid ever facing your feelings?

(4)

Start embracing uncertainty.

As we described when talking about grief and anxiety (see page 84), many people don't cope well with uncertainty, even in the best of times. Your loss has likely made everything feel uncertain, from your emotions to your future and your relationships. You can't just flip a switch and embrace the unpredictable nature of the future.

But you can do a few things to get more comfortable with uncertainty:

- Think back to uncertain times and emotions in the past that you weathered.
- Avoid dwelling and ruminating on things outside of your control.
- Lean on your support system as a reminder that you are not facing uncertainty alone.

- When emotions feel intense and uncertain, remember that emotions rise and fall. Instead of running from your emotions, you can choose to allow them to wash over you, knowing the feelings will pass.
- Keep practicing dialectical thinking (see page 193).
- Control what you can control—simple daily routines can go a long way when other aspects of life feel uncertain.

(5)

Start practicing curiosity.

This may not be your first loss. It might not even be the most complex loss you've navigated. But each loss you live through is new, bringing new emotions, new thoughts, new pain, new uncertainty, new questions, new fears. Layer all that on top of the loss itself, and it can feel overwhelming and terrifying. There is no easy answer for this, but one surprisingly helpful technique can be to get curious about each of these frightening new grief experiences. Observe the experience. Label it. Notice how it feels in your body. Notice your thoughts. Write about it. Draw about it. Seek to understand it, while also accepting that it may not be rational or comprehensible.

Use the following acceptance and commitment therapy (ACT) questions to observe your emotions in new and different ways (Hayes, 2009):

- If it had a color, what color would it be?
- If it had a size, how big would it be?
- If it had a shape, what shape would be?
- If it had a power, how much power would it have?
- If it had a speed, how fast would it go?
- If it had a texture, what would it feel like?

What's Your Grief Trigger?

A grief trigger is anything that brings up thoughts, emotions, and memories related to a loss. Triggers may be obvious and easy to anticipate, like the first holiday after a loss, or they may be surprising, such as spotting someone in a crowd who looks like your deceased loved one. A grief trigger might tie to a specific memory or emotion, or it may be something that flashes into consciousness and leaves you with a general sense of sadness and yearning.

Grief triggers are troubling because they open the floodgate for what are known in the mental health field as *involuntary autobiographical memories*. These pop into your head without any effort on your part to recall them. To clarify, these memories aren't entirely random and don't actually "come out of nowhere"; usually, a sight, sound, song, smell, or word triggers them. Many of these memories are harmless. But others, especially those associated with loss or trauma, can leave you feeling knocked over by a wave of grief.

Knowing that grief triggers exist can cause you a fair amount of anxiety. Aside from not wanting to feel terrible, there's the fear of triggers causing you to lose control emotionally, derailing your day, and setting you back in your grief.

So, how do you cope with grief triggers? First, understand that you *will* encounter grief triggers. Resist the temptation to avoid grief triggers altogether by staying locked in your room forever; this won't work, unfortunately. Instead, we suggest planning ahead for how you will handle grief triggers when they inevitably happen, both expectedly and unexpectedly.

Planning for unexpected grief triggers

It's impossible to anticipate every trigger you will ever encounter, so it's good to have a general way of coping with unexpected reminders of your loss. The tips we previously discussed for calming yourself down and getting comfortable with emotion are an excellent place to start (see pages 203 and 206). Additionally, keep the following in mind:

- **Your emotions can't hurt you.** You may experience anxiety and concern if you believe your emotions can harm you. Remind yourself that feelings cannot hurt you and that you are capable of handling them.

- **Don't be embarrassed.** Try not to feel ashamed of your emotions—especially if you're in public. It's unlikely that observers will judge you for your momentary outburst of emotion. Imagine seeing someone crying. Would you think, "That person is weak and stupid," or rather, "Been there, done that. They must be having a bad day."? We're guessing you'd think the latter.

- **Let your emotion wash over you.** Here's the thing about distressing emotions: they become intense, and then they usually dissipate. So if you allow yourself to experience the feeling, there's a good chance it will wash over you and recede.

- **Take some deep breaths.**

- **Take a break.** Give yourself ten minutes to get some fresh air or walk away from whatever you're doing.

Planning for expected grief triggers

Some triggers you can anticipate. When you know your triggers, big and small, you can think more specifically about how you will handle them. For example, imagine you have to go to a wedding shortly after breaking up with your fiancé. Knowing this experience could trigger grief, you might plan to bring your best friend as your plus-one for support, or you might come equipped with an excuse to leave early if everything gets to be too much.

So here's what we want you to do:

- Grab a sheet of paper or your journal and brainstorm some of the people, places, things, and experiences that could potentially trigger painful thoughts and difficult emotions. Are there triggers you've already been struggling with? Are there people or places you've been avoiding? Is there a special day or holiday coming up that you're worried might be difficult? Take a few minutes to write down anything you can think of—both expected triggers and potential unexpected one.

- Look at your list. Pick two or three triggers that seem the most imminent or likely to be encountered, and then take a few minutes to jot down a plan for coping with this trigger if and when it occurs.

9

Practices to Help You Reduce Worry and Rumination

Remember when we worried you about all the problematic consequences linked with rumination and then blew your mind by explaining that rumination is actually a form of avoidance? (If not, read the rumination list on page 94.) This list will help you cope with rumination and hopefully prevent those outcomes.

①

Practice accepting your thoughts rather than fighting them.

Sometimes the harder you try to stop thinking about something, the more you wind up thinking about it. This list is going to give you tools for accepting those hard thoughts instead of avoiding them, but the first step is to resolve to stop running from them and to using the tools below to face a specific thought the next time it bubbles up.

②

Learn to observe your thoughts.

This will feel really strange at first. But it can be a revolutionary practice. Start by remembering a thought is just a thought—no more, no less. It is the product of neurons firing in your brain. Your thoughts are sometimes true and sometimes untrue. Now, label the thoughts you are having. For example, when you notice yourself thinking, "I will never find a good job again," say to yourself, "I am having the thought that I will never find a good job again." This isn't about evaluating the thought. It isn't about judging. It is just about noticing. Labeling thoughts in this way is a good reminder that you exist separately from your thoughts—you can take a step back and observe them. Practice this regularly when worry arises by saying the following:

I am having the thought . . .
I am having the feeling of . . .

③
Watch your thoughts come in and go out.

Once you have become a bit better at observing your thoughts, you can practice techniques for watching the movement of your thoughts. This isn't about controlling your thoughts, just about observing how they come and go.

Try to imagine a thought you are having as an object that you can watch move. Maybe your thoughts are clouds in the sky, cars driving down a dirt road, leaves floating down a stream, balloons floating in the air— play around and find an image that works best for you. Whenever you observe a new, worrisome thought arising, label it, observe it, imagine it moving into your mind as that object, and then imagine it leaving your mind.

④
Set aside rumination time.

We know, this seems like a weird tip for helping you kick the rumination habit. But if a particular thought keeps coming up and you find yourself

what's your grief?

stuck on it, go ahead and dedicate some time to writing your thoughts in your journal or talking to a therapist. This can help you really look at the thought and figure out if it's something you can get comfortable with and stop ruminating about on your own, or if you need outside support.

Put the thought in a drawer (for now).

If your worry and rumination are creeping in at inopportune times, like during the workday or when you want to be present with friends and family, notice the thought and make a conscious choice to revisit it later. It can help to use a visualization technique to put the thought away until a later, less problematic time.

- Label the thought that you are having: "I am having the thoughts that Annie seems to be struggling in school because of the divorce and I don't know what to do for her."
- Set a specific time that you will return to this thought. We mean this literally— tell yourself exactly when you will return to it.
- Now imagine the thought as an object and give that object a place to go in your brain to wait until it is time. Some people like to visualize a "worry drawer" that's held closed with a lock. If you can't think of an object, visualize yourself writing the labeled thought on a piece of paper.
- Now imagine placing the object or piece of paper into the drawer, shut the drawer, lock it, and say to yourself, "This thought will stay right here until I come back to it later this evening."

Write it down.

There are many benefits to writing, so grab your journal if you haven't already. Just the act of writing down the thoughts and worries and reading them back can help you see your rumination differently. Writing can also help you see whether your thoughts and worries change at all, or whether you are simply rehashing the same things time and again. If the thoughts aren't changing, this might be a sign you could use some professional support.

(7)
Distract yourself.

By now you should be comfortable with the idea that a bit of healthy distraction is valuable in grief. When the usual thoughts you find yourself ruminating about creep in, have a list handy to remind yourself of your favorite distractions. Think of things that you enjoy, but that challenge you enough that it might snap your brain out of a rumination loop. Maybe it is cooking, crossword puzzles, video games, photography, woodworking, or anything else that can shift your thoughts and engage your senses.

(8)
Practice meditation.

One of the most challenging habits to break is your brain's pesky want to keep following intrusive thoughts, whether it serves you or not. Meditation is a practice that can, slowly but surely, train your brain to do something different and help you change your relationship with your thoughts. This is not an overnight fix for rumination. It is a slow process of training your brain to do something different. But beginning with a few minutes every day, listening to a guided meditation or using a meditation app, is a great place to start.

(9) Seek professional support.

Rumination can become a vicious cycle, one that is very hard to break. It can begin to feel comfortable even when it feels terrible. Though the tips above are a good place to start, if you aren't seeing any improvements, seek the help of a therapist for this one.

OTHER LISTS TO CHECK OUT:

5 Signs You Are Practicing Avoidance, page 81

6 Causes of Grief-Related Anxiety, page 84

5 Facts About Rumination, page 94

6

Suggestions for Living with Guilt and Regret

Guilt is the emotional response you have after committing a (real or perceived) moral transgression. When you believe you have done something wrong, you feel guilty.

Regret is related but different—it's simply when you wish something had turned out differently.

That's really all you need to know ahead of time to dig into coping with guilt and regret. But if those three sentences didn't ring any bells, we suggest you read the list on page 101 about guilt in grief before you continue. You'll be better off for it.

① Acknowledge that guilt has an important function.

Before we go further into coping with guilt, it is important to let go of any judgments you have about the feeling itself. Guilt lets you know you don't feel good about something you've done not so you get stuck in a cycle of shame and self-flagellation, but so you can do different next time.

Figure out whether you are feeling guilt, regret, or both.

(2)

Regret, as we've defined above, has nothing to do with whether you caused the event you wish hadn't happened, intended it, or had anything to do with it at all! Guilt is the feeling that comes up when you believe that you did something wrong. There are three big reasons that people feel guilt that can help you assess which one you're feeling:

1. You really did something hurtful and wrong.
2. You believe you did something hurtful and wrong (but you didn't).
3. Your seeking order and control (so you'd rather blame yourself than admit that sometimes the world is unpredictable and uncontrollable).

The distinction between guilt and regret is important, so if you have certain guilt and regret stuck points, it can be helpful to really look at them closely and talk them through with someone.

(3)

Practice the thought and feeling observation technique on page 213.

Once you've determined the thoughts you're having and the feelings of guilt or regret associated with them, label and examine them.

Assess whether hindsight bias is impacting your guilt.

As we described on page 120, hindsight bias is a normal and common psychological phenomenon that causes people to believe that outcomes of past events were predictable, even though they weren't. When considering something you're feeling guilty about, go back to the time of the event and try to remember exactly what you knew and what you didn't know. Try to recall what your motivation and intention was at the time. Most importantly, try not to use information about the outcome or things you learned later. This can be tough to do, but it will help you to more accurately appraise the past situation and your actions.

(5)

Ask yourself if you're engaging in counterfactual thinking.

Counterfactual thinking is another one of those mind tricks that we shared earlier (see page 120). Counterfactual thinking is the cause of a lot of "what if . . ." and "if only . . ." thinking. Consider your own thinking about a situation for which you feel guilt or regret. Are you assuming that, had things gone differently, the outcome would have definitely been a favorable one? Oftentimes that is the assumption, when the reality is that you can only know that things would have been different. You have no way to know for sure if the alternate outcome would have been better, worse, or exactly the same.

Determine what you've learned from your guilt or regret—and what you'll do with those lessons.

Though people will tell you not to indulge feelings like guilt and regret, the truth is that getting down and dirty with these feelings is valuable; it allows you the opportunity to understand them, learn, forgive yourself, and grow. Honestly, what kind of a person would you be if every time you made a mistake you shrugged your shoulders and forgot about it? Survey says . . . a crappy person! Considering exactly what your guilt and regret have taught you and how they will inform the person you are going forward is crucial. For more on this, see page 223.

OTHER LISTS TO CHECK OUT:

Understanding Hindsight Bias and Counterfactual Thinking

If you're having a hard time understanding hindsight bias and counter-factual thinking, an example can help. Imagine that your partner died of an unexpected heart attack while on a business trip. After her death you replay everything that happened, telling friends, "She said she wasn't feeling well the morning she left. I should have known something serious was wrong and taken her to the doctor. If I'd encouraged her to stay home she'd still be alive." Your belief that you should have interpreted casual complaints about not feeling well as something serious comes from your knowing the outcome and from your brain seeking evidence that there was something predictable and preventable. In reality, your partner had no preexisting conditions and there was absolutely no indication that this was any more serious than the dozens of other times in the course of your relationship that she mentioned not feeling well.

The suggestion that she would have survived had she not gone on the trip is predicated on a belief that had she stayed home, you would have convinced her to go to the doctor, the doctor would have caught the heart attack, you would have been there to start CPR, or some other imagined story that allows you to believe that you could have had the outcome you wished for. Unfortunately, there is simply no way to know. She may have stayed home and not gone to the doctor, or the doctor might not have detected it, or you might not have been home when the heart attack happened, or your CPR might have been unsuccessful, or any number of other potential outcomes.

Part of the reason we engage in these patterns of thinking is that, though they lead to self-blame, they allow us a perception of control. Believing that you could have predicted your partner's heart attack and prevented it might lead to self-blame and guilt, but that might be pref-erable to the reality that sometimes people die from undetectable and unpreventable health conditions.

9

Suggestions for Finding Self-Forgiveness (and Making Amends)

Just because you feel guilty doesn't mean you are guilty, so before reading this list, please make sure you assess your guilt and regret with the information on page 218.

Once you have identified the things for which you were truly responsible and want to forgive yourself or make amends, settle in. This process can be tough.

(1)

Consider the difference between guilt and shame.

We all screw up. Sometimes our screw-ups are small, sometimes they are huge, sometimes they are devastating. But doing a bad thing is different from being a bad person. Though each of your actions carries ethical weight, no single action defines who you are. A single good deed does not define you as a good person, and a single mistake does not define you as a bad person. And you may think this only impacts the way you see yourself, but research has shown that those who feel guilt rather than shame are less likely to make the same mistakes in the future (Maruna, 2000).

Know what self-forgiveness means—
and what it doesn't mean.

Sometimes people hesitate to seek self-forgiveness because they think that it means letting themselves off the hook or denying their wrongdoing. It doesn't. Though there are different definitions of forgiveness, the one we prefer is from the Human Development Study Group and the University in Wisconsin: "a willingness to abandon one's right to resentment, negative judgment, and indifferent behavior to one who unjustly injured us, while fostering the undeserved qualities of compassion, generosity and even love toward him or her" (Enright et al. in Enright and North, 1998). But because we are talking about self-forgiveness here, that "him or her" is you! They go on to say "we still see [him or her] as the perpetrator of the wrong and the one who is responsible for it. . . . There must be a real sense of the wrongdoer as responsible and the wrong as real if forgiveness is to be meaningful at all. After all, if there is no wrong and no wrongdoer, then there is nothing and no one to forgive."

Working on self-forgiveness means moving closer to abandoning your right to resentment, negative judgment, and indifferent behavior *toward yourself* while fostering the undeserved qualities of compassion, generosity and even love *toward yourself*. This is not rewriting the past to say what you did wasn't wrong; it is forgiving yourself *because* you did something wrong.

Consider whether you are holding yourself
to a different standard.

Would you forgive a friend or family member in the same situation? Would you tell them to forgive themselves? If so, consider why you are treating yourself differently. What allows you to forgive that person and not yourself?

(4)

Forget about asking for forgiveness;
this is about self-forgiveness.

When you ask someone to forgive you, you're asking them to do work. Making an apology and making amends is when *you* do the work. So for now, set aside the idea of wanting forgiveness from anyone else. You cannot control whether another person decides to forgive you or not (especially if that person has died!). What you can control are your actions, grounded in your values.

(5)

Make a direct amends.

Making amends is *doing* something to compensate or make up for wrongdoing. In some cases, you will be able to make amends by directly righting a wrong, and if you are lucky enough to be able to do that, we encourage you to get to it. (If not, see #7 below.) Your amends cannot be contingent on someone else's willingness to forgive you. You should take action without the expectation of their forgiveness and, rather, because it is the right thing to do. Go to the person, take responsibility for your wrongdoing, ask if there is something you can do to make it up to them, and be ready with your own ideas of what you may be able to do.

(6)

Apologize.

Part of righting a wrong often includes taking ownership of that wrong. That often takes the shape of an apology. According to Oxford Languages, an apology is "a regretful acknowledgment of an offense or failure." When you are apologizing, be forthright, take responsibility, and express directly how you will work to prevent the same thing from happening again.

Avoid being defensive but conversely don't wallow in excessive remorse or belaboring the emotional toll the guilt has taken on you. Like amends, an apology is not a request for forgiveness. When you apologize, you are giving something to the person you have wronged. When you seek forgiveness, you are asking another to give you something.

Remember, although you may feel ready to rehash the past and lay all your wrongdoings on the table, others may not be emotionally ready to do so, especially in grief. In instances such as these, it may only make sense to extend an olive branch and allow the healing to continue over time. Your healing cannot come at the expense of someone else's well-being. That would totally defeat the purpose!

⑦

Make a living amends.

A direct amends, unfortunately, is not always possible. The circumstances may simply not lend themselves to a direct amends, time may have passed, someone may have died or cut off contact with you. When you cannot directly make up for something to the person you hurt, a living amends is a decision to change your ongoing behavior in a way that is informed by the wrongdoing. You make a living amends by living in a way that acknowledges the previous mistake by consistently choosing not to repeat it or by compensating for it.

Imagine that you deeply regret not visiting your grandmother more often while she was still living. Unfortunately, you cannot make a direct amends for this—she's gone. You can recognize that your behavior violated values that are important to you, like prioritizing time with family. Taking ownership of your actions and making a conscious decision that going forward you will choose the value of time with family above other competing priorities can serve as a living amends.

(8)

Actively decide to forgive yourself.

This does not mean excusing yourself for your past wrongdoings. It means going through the steps above, showing yourself self-compassion, and making a conscious decision to let go of the self-judgment, criticism, and resentment you have toward yourself. Remember, to err is human.

(9)

Seek professional support.

Guilt and shame can be relentless. If, despite your best efforts, you find yourself stuck in a cycle of guilt and unable to forgive yourself, seeking professional help is an important next step.

OTHER LISTS TO CHECK OUT:

6 Suggestions for Living with Guilt and Regret, page 218

Make Your Own List: What's Your Grief Secret?, page 110

5 Reactions You May Have to a Chaotic and Uncontrollable World, page 88

What Are Your Grief Support Needs?

Identifying your needs after a loss can be harder than you'd expect. Like so many things in grief, the needs you'll experience after a loss are often complex and diverse. They may change from day to day, week to week, and month to month.

It's only logical that in order to get help meeting your needs, you need to first figure out what those needs are. Some of your needs will be obvious to you; others less so. Some will be concrete and tangible, others will be more abstract. To determine your needs, it can be helpful to consider nine domains that are commonly impacted.

- Emotional needs

- Spiritual needs

- Practical needs

- Physical or health-related needs

- Mental health and well-being needs

- Financial needs

- Remembrance needs

- Creativity needs

- Relationship needs

Note that you may have needs that fall outside these domains. It can also be helpful to consider what would allow you to feel more supported in moments of intense emotion.

So here's what we want you to do:

- Consider the nine domains commonly impacted by grief. If you're struggling in any of these areas, it's likely that you have some grief support needs.

- On a sheet of paper or in your journal, create a column or section for each of these domains.

- Spend ten minutes or so writing down any support needs you can think of—big and small—that fall under each column.

Keep this list close at hand as a reference and try to remember to add to it when new needs arise. It will help guide you in thinking about whom you might reach out to for support with specific needs.

3

To-Dos for Utilizing Your Support System

"Let me know if there's anything I can do."

You've probably heard the phrase dozens of times since experiencing the loss that brought you to this book.

Expert advice suggests that those wishing to support someone going through hardship should not make such generalized offers because it puts the burden on you, the person struggling, to identify your needs and ask for help. As we covered on page 228, identifying your needs is hard enough. For many, asking for or accepting help is even harder.

Though it is good advice to offer specific support, many people hesitate to make such offers. They don't know what you need or they don't want to overstep your boundaries. Sadly this often leaves those struggling after a loss and those who want to help at an impasse.

If there is to be hope of moving forward from that impasse, sometimes it falls to you to figure out how to best enlist your support system. (Annoying, we know.) As a person struggling with a loss, the last thing you want to do is figure out how to help people help you. But the reality is that no one got a manual for this—not you, not them. So a little can go a long way. What do we mean?

① Figure out what you need.

Great news! Assuming you're reading this book in order, you just did that in the last list. If you didn't, go to page 228 and read that list before you move on.

② Get comfortable asking for help.

Many of us were raised with a sense of rugged individualism that has become a nagging little voice in our heads. It says things like, "Buck up," "Stay strong," or "You should be able to figure out how to do this on your own." Remember how we've established that your thoughts aren't always true? This is a key moment to remind yourself of that again.

Friendships and relationships are about being there for each other. If you knew one of your friends was struggling and there was something you could do to help, our guess is that you would want to do it. If you learned they weren't asking because they felt like a burden, you'd probably be upset. Take a moment to consider—really consider—that your friends and family may feel the same way about you.

③ Identify the best person to help you with your needs.

Everyone has their own unique strengths and weaknesses. Some people are good listeners, some are good advice givers, and some are great for comic relief.

Think of your friends and family as a toolkit. It's important to find the right tool for a job based on a person's unique characteristics (personality, strengths, abilities, etc.). All people cannot be all things to you, and that's okay. It doesn't always mean they're a bad friend. It just means they are really great for some things, and not so great for others.

When you turn to someone for a type of support they are not equipped to give, you set that person up for failure, and you set yourself for disappointment.

To help you match the people in your life with the type of grief support they are best equipped to offer, we have an activity we call Support System Superlatives. Remember the superlatives handed out in your high school yearbook like Best Dressed and Most Likely to Succeed? We want you to decide who in your support system is "most likely" to meet your grief support needs. Who's most likely to listen without judgment, most likely to help you with carpool, or most likely to tell you the ugly truth?

As you do this activity, think beyond your support system's first tier to people, professionals, and organizations in your community. Your next-door neighbor, whom you only casually know, might not be the person to open up to about the emotional impact of your recent lupus diagnosis. But she may absolutely win Most Likely to Help Me Dig My Car Out of the Snow When My Body Won't Cooperate.

OTHER LISTS TO CHECK OUT:

Make Your Own List: What Are Your Grief Support Needs?, page 228

5 Ws to Help You Understand Support Systems, page 51

5 Reasons It Can Feel Like Your Grief Has Been Forgotten, page 142

9

Tips for Communicating What You Do (and Don't) Need

Knowing what you need (and don't need) and whom to ask can feel much easier than actually expressing those needs. On top of that, some people in your life may be "supporting" you in ways that feel legitimately harmful, like saying or doing things that feel minimizing or pushy. You know you need to tell them how their behavior impacts you, but you aren't sure how. Regardless of the topic, the following steps can help you navigate these sometimes awkward and often complex discussions.

Describe what you have observed about your own needs and experiences.

This doesn't have to be complicated; simply describe what you have been feeling and experiencing.

> *"Since my divorce, I have been feeling lonely but also isolating myself because I don't have much energy to do things. It has been hard."*

(2)

State what you think would be helpful.

Again, a simple description of your needs can go a long way.

"Because my motivation is so low, I think it would really help me for other people to coordinate plans and invite me, rather than it falling on me to reach out."

(3)

Make a specific ask.

Be direct and just ask for exactly what you need.

"Would you be able to coordinate a few things for us to do over the next few weeks? And if I try to back out, will you be gentle but still at least push me a little bit?"

See, not too painful, right? The conversation might seem more difficult if you're communicating with someone who hurt you, but the steps above can still work incredibly well.

(4)

Ask others to help you communicate your needs.

It can be daunting to imagine telling friends and family what you need. If one or two trusted people have asked what they can do to help, let them know your needs and what is and isn't working in your support system. Then ask them to speak with other friends and family on your behalf.

5

Set boundaries.

Sometimes, no matter how fantastic your communication is about what you need and what you don't, some people continue to disregard what you've told them. Maybe they're not capable of meeting your needs; maybe they don't want to. Whatever the reason, you may ultimately need to set boundaries with these people.

To put it simply, a boundary is a limit you set between you and another person. It often creates an important physical or emotional space that helps you maintain your well-being within the relationship. Boundaries can be set around your time, communication, physical space, finances, intimacy, and almost anything else that protects your energy and resources. Some common grief boundaries include setting limits on topics you will discuss, when and how people visit you, and offers and requests for assistance.

6

Communicate your boundaries.

Once you know your boundaries, you need to tell the other person simply and directly what the boundary is. Then let them know the consequence for not respecting it. If setting boundaries is new to you, this might sound harsh. But in fact it will allow everyone to be on the same page. Imagine your sister keeps talking to you about starting to date, even after you've repeatedly said that you feel rushed and asked her to stop and instead to take her cues from you. You might set a boundary like this:

> *"Megan, I've mentioned to you that I needed people to take their cues from me about when I will start dating, yet you keep bringing it up. I love you, I understand that you are trying to help, and I value our relationship. But in order for us to*

*continue talking regularly, you cannot bring up dating with me
at all anymore. This is really important to me and if you can't
respect this, I am going to have to end any conversation when
you bring it up and start limiting our interaction to maintain
my own mental well-being."*

⑦

Know your needs and boundaries can change.

What you need now might not be what you need in six months, and that's
okay. You can always communicate as your needs and boundaries shift.
Continue being open to the questions that this brings up from friends and
family, knowing that it can be very hard for them to understand your grief
until you give them insight into your experience and emotions.

⑧

Tell people what you're looking for from them
(and what you're not looking for).

In grief, others are often unsure what to do to help, and this includes in
conversation. Going to the right person for the right thing is important,
but it can also help to let people know from the outset what you're looking
for from them. It is really basic and sounds something like this:

- "I had a really hard day today at work after someone asked about Josh.
  Can I tell you about it? I don't want you to try to cheer me up or fix it, I just
  really need someone to listen."
- "I've been feeling really anxious about some stuff related to the divorce.
  At this point, I can't tell if I am overreacting or not. Can I tell you about it
  and get your opinion?"

$$\textbf{(9)}$$

Learn to say no.

For all the people-pleasers out there, for all who try to avoid making others uncomfortable, for those who think they are responsible for other people's comfort at all times—this is your permission to say no. It is okay to:

- Tell someone you don't want to talk about it when they ask questions about your loss or anything else that you simply don't want to talk about.
- Decline someone's offer of support if it isn't the support you need.
- Say no to an invitation or cancel plans if you simply aren't up for it.
- Explain that your bandwidth is low, so you aren't in a position to take on anything extra (at work, volunteering, with family or friends, etc.).

OTHER LISTS TO CHECK OUT:

Make Your Own List: What Are Your Grief Support Needs?, page 228

7 Steps to Help You Live According to Your Values, page 167

Make Your Own List: What's Your Anti-Loneliness Wish List?, page 134

5

Questions to Ask Yourself Before Writing Someone Off

People say and do the wrong things sometimes. This is annoying at the best of times and deeply hurtful at the worst. It can feel like a total failure of empathy from the people you trusted to be there for you. Sometimes it is a failure of empathy, but sometimes people are just unsure of what to say or do.

Though it can be tempting to write someone off when they haven't been there for you when you needed them, the links between social support, health, and healing (both physical and emotional) are too compelling for us to let you walk away from all of your family and friends. That said, the next logical question is, when is enough enough? When is a person beyond second chances? The answers to these questions are complicated and dependent on the situation. But the following questions can help you decide if it's time to start cutting your losses with certain people in your life.

(1)

What were their intentions?

When people say or do the wrong thing, often they have good intentions but they don't quite stick the landing. They rush you because they don't want you to be sad or suffering anymore. They look for a silver lining. They try to connect with you, but in doing so they make things about themselves. When someone says the wrong thing, take a minute to reflect on their intention, and see if you can have a little more empathy for them (hard when they have just said something awful, we know). Considering their intentions can also help you assess where this misstep falls in the big picture of your relationship.

Have I acknowledged that my pain is valid, even if their intention was not to cause pain?

If you felt hurt by someone, that is a valid feeling. Their intentions don't diminish your pain. You can be empathetic to their intentions without giving them a pass. Letting the hurt slide because their intentions weren't malicious doesn't help them become a better support person to you or to others. So hold both truths at once: they didn't mean to hurt you, but they did hurt you.

Have I given them feedback?

We know, when you're already suffering and just want support, giving someone feedback that they're being unsupportive is miserable. Our backgrounds are in mental health and we still dread this type of interpersonal awkwardness. But people who find ways to give their friends and family feedback end up having more responsive and supportive friends and family members. And the bottom line is this: if you don't tell someone they've hurt you, they can't apologize, fix it, or do better next time. If you do communicate with them and they make no effort to fix the problem, then you've learned something important about them. Ultimately, if you need to take a break from the relationship, you have peace of mind of knowing that you gave them a chance before calling it quits.

(4)

Can I preserve this relationship if I set some boundaries?

Sometimes your decision to write someone off isn't because they disappeared or said the wrong thing. Sometimes it is because they keep getting overly involved. Perhaps they give you advice, ask you questions you aren't comfortable with, or come over unannounced to check in. Before you write off this well-intentioned person who is just taking up too much space, consider whether setting some boundaries might help.

(5)

Is it worth one more chance, or is it enough?

If you're sure you've expressed your needs, given feedback, and set your boundaries and this person is still failing you or using energy that you need for yourself, it might be time for a break. You may find you've outgrown the relationship for good. Or you can reconnect with them later, when you're feeling stronger. Dialectical thinking can be important here (see page 193).

OTHER LISTS TO CHECK OUT:

9 Tips for Communicating What You Do (and Don't) Need, page 233

8 Misconceptions About Blame, Anger, and Forgiveness, page 244

10 Types of Stigmatizing Statements, page 108

5
Things to Remember When a Friendship Ends

You might be reading this book because your primary loss is the end of a friendship. Or because whatever other loss brought you to this book led to losing other relationships. Grief, no matter what the type of loss, can rewrite your address book.

Sometimes your needs and friendship values change, especially during times of loss and life transitions. Some friendships simply cannot withstand those shifts. Here are some important reminders to help you cope with the unique challenges of losing a friend.

① Consider some of the most common reasons friendships end.

This is far from an exhaustive list, but it can be helpful to remember that your friendship is not the only friendship that has suffered this painful fate.

- One person changed in ways the friendship couldn't tolerate. This comes when someone joins or leaves a religion, joins or leaves a cult, changes their personality for a new romantic relationship, or enters drug or alcohol recovery.
- When a friend doesn't know what to do in a crisis or with the other person's grief, they offer bad support or disappear altogether.

- Even with the best of intentions, sometimes moving or leaving a job means a friend loses touch.
- After one friend goes through a divorce or loses a loved one, the other friend distances themselves.
- Grieving people sometimes feel they've outgrown or drifted away from certain friendships.

Give yourself permission to grieve the person and what they meant to you.

It is obvious that you miss your friend and your time with them, but don't forget that there are often secondary losses within this loss.

- The loss of someone with who you share memories and a history with
- The loss of their role in your family or friend group
- The loss of the other roles they filled in your life, such as advice giver, cheerleader, or shoulder to cry on
- The loss of who you were when you were with them

Know that a friendship's end does not nullify the quality and value of the relationship while it lasted.

Sad as it may be, people come and go from our lives. A friendship doesn't have to be forever to have been worthwhile. The end of the relationship doesn't have to override the good stuff at the beginning and the middle. Now, we aren't naive. We get it that sometimes the end feels so egregious and revealing that it changes how you view everything. If there was hurt or betrayal, that can be hard to look past. But at least give yourself space to consider the possibility that the friendship had value and served you while it lasted.

what's your grief?

(4)

Remember, this friendship ending isn't a reason to question all your other friendships.

When one friendship ends, you may realize that friendships can be more fragile than they feel. Your trust for others might plummet as you start wondering whether other friends might disappear, go through a personality change, or fail you. You might even find yourself questioning your ability to appraise people and friendships. Remember, one friendship is one friendship. People change, and there is no reason to believe that because one relationship has come to a close, others will follow suit.

(5)

Rituals can help.

This doesn't have to be anything big or fancy. But if you realize this friendship is over, at least for the foreseeable future, it can help to say goodbye. This isn't the same as closure; your grief won't end here. But a private, personal ritual is a way to say to yourself: *I am grieving this loss, I am moving forward with the things this friendship gave me, but leaving the friendship itself behind.*

OTHER LISTS TO CHECK OUT:

7 Types of Grief You Should Know (but Probably Don't), page 28

6 Things to Understand About Anger, page 127

6 Reasons Loss Creates Conflict with Others, page 131

8

Misconceptions About Blame, Anger, and Forgiveness

> *"I know anger isn't sustainable, but I'm afraid to feel the sadness—it's protecting. My anger is control, it gives me say. My sadness knows I have neither."*
>
> —NADIA BOWERS, IN HER 2018 *TIME* MAGAZINE ESSAY "WHAT I'D SAY TO THE DRUG DEALER WHO GAVE MY SISTER A FATAL DOSE OF HEROIN"

Though we've talked about why anger is so common in grief, it still leaves the looming question of what to do with all that anger and blame. Examining misunderstandings and myths about feeling anger and seeking forgiveness is a surprisingly helpful place to start.

①

Anger and blame are always the product of wrongdoing.

We've said before that blame often comes up because it is human nature to want a reason *why* bad things happen. This allows people a sense of order. If someone screwed up, if someone was to blame, then we feel safer in the belief that it won't happen unexpectedly again. People will often place blame for even the most senseless and disordered of things, because it gives a feeling of control. When we say *people*, this includes you. Look at your anger and blame and assess where wanting order and control might be impacting you.

② It's wrong to feel angry.

Like other feelings and emotions, anger isn't inherently good or bad. It isn't something to be judged or avoided or even "managed." When anger arises, you can notice and observe with curiosity. Anger serves a biological function, and feeling it is part of the full range of human emotional experience. The problem is not that you feel anger; the problem is if you let that anger consume or guide you in a way that takes you further from the person that you want to be and the life you want to live.

③ Accepting anger means being angry.

When you notice anger, you have a choice to make. In what direction will your anger take you?

There is a fork in the road that people commonly come to in grief. To the left is the road of acting on anger, blame, and rumination and letting these guide your choices. To the right, the road of acting on your values.

Both paths allow you to feel your anger, to accept and experience it when it comes up. But on the first path you will "be" angry, in the sense that anger will guide you. On the second, you will feel and experience anger, but you will make conscious choices not to allow your anger to consume you, instead allowing other values to lead the way.

$$\textbf{4}$$

To live in accordance with your values, you must stop feeling angry.

If you decide to take the values path (and we hope that you do), you will probably need to practice connecting with and accepting anger while not being guided by it. It takes effort to do this. You can start by approaching your anger with compassion and gentle awareness while developing a deeper connection to your values, which *will* guide you forward.

Imagine, for example, that you've been deeply hurt by your partner's infidelity, which ultimately led to your divorce. Your anger is still raw and deep and you don't want to speak with him, but there are logistics involving your children that you need to discuss. All you can hear is the voice in your head screaming, "I can't believe he would do this to our family, I am so angry, I'm simply not going to speak with him!" And then you notice the feeling and label it: "I am having the feeling of anger." You're filled with pain and betrayal, which you might also label.

When you accept those emotions, you can say to yourself, "I am feeling those emotions, but I don't have to act on them unless I choose to. So though I am deeply angry, coparenting and family are critical values for me. I am going to make an active decision to follow the path of coparenting and family, rather than anger, and call my ex to discuss this issue."

$$\textbf{5}$$

Anger hurts other people more than it hurts you.

Anger can come from true hurt and betrayal. Acting on anger often feels like a tool for hurting another person or allowing them to experience some of your pain. The want to hurt the other person can overshadow the reality that anger hurts *you* over time. Let's be honest, anger is draining. Even when it is not guiding your behaviors, it can consume your thoughts, impact your worldview, and spill over into other areas of your life.

⑥

Forgiveness is for the perpetrator.

Forgiveness releases *you* of the anger and resentment that can leave *you* unhappy. This can sound cliché, but it is true. It is something you can decide to do for yourself, not for the perpetrator. We're not just making this stuff up. A meta-analysis of fifty-four studies on forgiveness found that people who forgave others consistently reduced their own depression, anxicty, and increased hope (Wade et al., 2014).

⑦

Forgiveness is about condoning or forgetting.

The Human Development Study Group at the University of Wisconsin developed the definition of forgiveness that we find the most useful. They define forgiveness as "a willingness to abandon one's right to resentment, negative judgment, and indifferent behavior to one who unjustly injured us, while fostering the undeserved qualities of compassion, generosity and even love toward him or her" (Enright et al. in Enright and North, 1998). Some important points here: they say you have a *right* to your resentment. They say your decision to forgive is *undeserved*. Why? Because forgiveness doesn't mean absolving the other person of wrongdoing or condoning what happened. It means accepting what they did was wrong and forgiving them anyway.

⑧

You have to navigate forgiveness on your own.

Forgiveness is not something that you decide to do and then suddenly it happens. It is a slow process and there are several different evidence-based approaches that can guide you. Walking you through them is beyond the scope of this book (because forgiveness is complicated). But the two we recommend you check out, because they are backed up by substantial research, are the Enright Forgiveness Process Model and the Worthington REACH Forgiveness Model (Wade et al., 2014).

OTHER LISTS TO CHECK OUT:

6 Things to Understand About Anger, page 127

4 Tips for Finding Calm in Your Grief Storm, page 203

5 Reactions You May Have to a Chaotic and Uncontrollable World, page 88

27

Things to Help You Feel Less Isolated

Loneliness and isolation have the ability to erode both your emotional and your physical well-being. Feeling cut off from social interaction can trigger a spiral of negative thinking about oneself (I have nothing to offer others, I'm not interesting, I'm different) and about others (everyone lies, no one understands me).

When you're lonely your brain tries to find reasons why, and sometimes the answers it comes up with are less than logical. For example, rather than thinking, "I'm going through a tough adjustment period," you might think, "I don't fit in anywhere." Assumptions like this become confused with facts and the next time you work up the courage to leave the house, you are more inclined to see the world through this negative lens.

As if the emotional toll weren't enough, one only needs to google *loneliness* to find that it's linked to a slew of physical maladies such as hardening of the arteries, high blood pressure, inflammation, problems with learning and memory, immune system suppression, increase in the stress hormone cortisol, lower quality of sleep, and premature aging. Yikes!

Isolation is a health risk, so it's important to pay attention to how you're coping in the weeks and months following a loss, especially if you're someone who tends to withdraw into oneself. If you see yourself slipping into isolation, it's probably best to try and find a few small ways to connect. We'll get you started with these techniques.

1 RECOGNIZE NEGATIVE THINKING AND THE STORIES YOU ARE TELLING YOURSELF.

2 TRY INDIVIDUAL OR GROUP THERAPY.

3 DECIDE THAT CONNECTION AND RELATIONSHIPS ARE WORTH PRIORITIZING.

4 DON'T MINIMIZE YOUR ISOLATION.

5 ASK FOR HELP.

6 TELL PEOPLE THAT YOU'RE ISOLATING.

7 WRITE AN EMAIL, SEND A SOCIAL MEDIA MESSAGE, TEXT A FAMILY MEMBER, SEND A LETTER, OR PHONE A FRIEND.

8 EASE BACK IN SLOWLY AND BE SELECTIVE.

9 SAY HELLO, SMILE, OR MAKE EYE CONTACT WHEN WALKING DOWN THE STREET.

10 REMEMBER THAT SOMETIMES YOU NEED TO DO THINGS YOU DON'T WANT TO DO.

what's your grief?

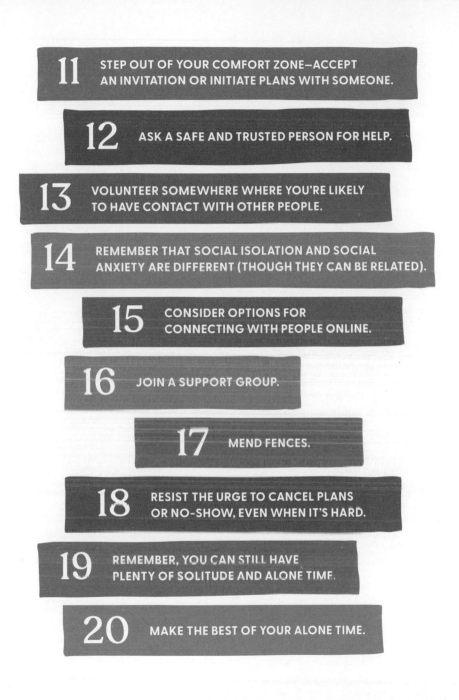

11 STEP OUT OF YOUR COMFORT ZONE—ACCEPT AN INVITATION OR INITIATE PLANS WITH SOMEONE.

12 ASK A SAFE AND TRUSTED PERSON FOR HELP.

13 VOLUNTEER SOMEWHERE WHERE YOU'RE LIKELY TO HAVE CONTACT WITH OTHER PEOPLE.

14 REMEMBER THAT SOCIAL ISOLATION AND SOCIAL ANXIETY ARE DIFFERENT (THOUGH THEY CAN BE RELATED).

15 CONSIDER OPTIONS FOR CONNECTING WITH PEOPLE ONLINE.

16 JOIN A SUPPORT GROUP.

17 MEND FENCES.

18 RESIST THE URGE TO CANCEL PLANS OR NO-SHOW, EVEN WHEN IT'S HARD.

19 REMEMBER, YOU CAN STILL HAVE PLENTY OF SOLITUDE AND ALONE TIME.

20 MAKE THE BEST OF YOUR ALONE TIME.

21 IF YOU DON'T HAVE A STRONG SUPPORT SYSTEM TO RECONNECT WITH, INTENTIONALLY PLACE YOURSELF IN SOCIAL SETTINGS JUST TO BE AROUND PEOPLE.

22 ASK PEOPLE ABOUT THEMSELVES.

23 LOOK FOR EVIDENCE IN YOUR ENVIRONMENT THAT YOU AREN'T ACTUALLY ALONE.

24 LOOK FOR SIMILARITIES IN OTHERS, RATHER THAN DIFFERENCES.

25 JOIN A CLUB OR GROUP WHERE PEOPLE HAVE SIMILAR INTERESTS TO YOUR OWN.

26 IF ONE NEW PERSON OR GROUP DOESN'T WORK FOR YOU, DON'T WRITE OFF ALL PEOPLE OR GROUPS. TRY ANOTHER.

27 AVOID UNHEALTHY RELATIONSHIPS, AT LEAST UNTIL YOU'RE IN A BETTER PLACE TO WORK ON THEM AND SET BOUNDARIES.

OTHER LISTS TO CHECK OUT:

3 To-Dos for Utilizing Your Support System, page 230

Make Your Own List: What's Your Anti-Loneliness Wish List?, page 134

8 Risk Factors for Experiencing Isolation, page 135

6

Suggestions to Help You Embrace Being Alone

You can be surrounded by other people and still feel lonely. You can also be alone while not experiencing loneliness. We can't know how you're feeling at the moment—lonely or not. But we do know that living with a loss puts you at a greater chance of being alone. Be it a breakup, divorce, death of a partner, relocation, or any number of other losses, grief can leave you feeling more isolated from others.

In addition to coping with social isolation (see page 249), getting more comfortable with being alone is a skill that can be learned. If you've lived with a partner, family member, or roommate for years, the shift to living alone can be difficult. The best way to support your well-being is a mix of strategies for decreasing isolation coupled with skills to embrace being alone, including the following.

①

Take yourself out.

You don't need a friend or partner to go to a restaurant, movie, museum, play, basketball game, or anywhere else. If going out alone is outside your comfort zone, ease your way in slowly; start by visiting familiar or comforting places, and then expand beyond them as you become more comfortable venturing out.

(2)

Love your space.

If living alone is new to you and you have the luxury of time or money to make your space more comfortable for you, do it. Enlist a friend or professional to help you if inspiration is high but motivation is low. One of the perks of living alone is that you make all the rules. Rearrange the furniture, paint, buy art you're excited about, splurge on nice speakers if you love music or movies, or upgrade to fancy new pots and pans if you like to cook. You get the idea.

(3)

Fight the urge to distract.

If you find the silence of being alone deafening, the logical response is to fill it with noise. You might find yourself with the TV, radio, music, or podcasts streaming in the background at all times just to keep you from being alone with the silence and your thoughts. Though a little healthy distraction and avoidance can be a great way to cope, learning to be alone with yourself is also important. It might be uncomfortable at first, but start with at least a few minutes of fully present, quiet, alone time each day.

(4)

Consider a pet (responsibly).

Remember that pets require time, energy, and money, so make sure you're ready for the commitment before taking this step. But if an empty house coupled with loneliness is starting to get to you, a fur friend can be a loving, comforting addition to your household—as long as you're fully capable to take on this responsibility. Pets shouldn't entirely replace human interaction but are a wonderful middle ground.

⑤
Try new hobbies.

It isn't that you can't do this when you live with someone. But limited time and shared space made picking up a new hobby harder when you're not alone. Choose things you used to enjoy or try something completely new. There's no one to judge you if your guitar skills aren't great or complain that your model train set runs through the dining room, so the sky's the limit.

Travel.

Depending on your comfort level, simply going to a baseball game, restaurant, or movie alone can be a big deal. But once you've become comfortable with doing those things solo in your hometown, you're only a small step away from traveling on your own. If the thought makes you nervous, start with a destination where you've been before, somewhere not too far away, or a place where you know someone. You can also join a travel group as a first step to traveling without anyone you know, while still being with other people.

OTHER LISTS TO CHECK OUT:

Make Your Own List: What's in Your Coping Bucket?, page 185

7 Steps to Help You Cope When You Don't Feel Like Coping, page 196

Make Your Own List: What's Your Reasons to Live List?, page 273

4

Places to Look for Grief Support in Your Community

Think about the tier of your support system that exists beyond your friends and family, the tier of support made up of people, groups, and organizations in your community who provide formal-ish support and assistance. Some examples include people and groups like support groups, therapists, childcare providers, coaches, clubs, doctors, and accountants.

In this list, we will focus specifically on people and groups in this tier that can offer you grief support. Taking steps to access this kind of support can be intimidating for many reasons, and we understand that you may feel hesitant. However, we want to encourage you to consider strengthening this layer of support because there are many benefits to interacting in spaces where there's the expectation of personal disclosure, shared experiences, mutual support, nonjudgment, and, in some cases, confidentiality. In addition, seeking community support may be especially important if you don't have many friends or relatives you can talk to about your grief and loss.

①

Seek therapy (or teletherapy).

Finding the right therapist is a bit like dating; not all therapists will be a good fit for you. You have to ask questions to get a good feel for the person's education, training, style, and approach. We typically recommend finding a licensed therapist with specific experience and training in working with grieving people. One caveat is, if your loss involves an issue or experience that complicates your ability to cope with grief, like trauma or addiction, we first recommend finding someone who specializes in those areas.

②

Look for support groups related to your specific loss (divorce, infertility, addiction, death of a loved one).

Word-of-mouth recommendations are an excellent place to start. However, a Google search will also help point you toward options in your area if they exist.

If you are grieving the death of a loved one, check with local hospices, which usually offer at least a general support group. Check other local organizations like hospitals, or houses of worship if you are open to something faith based. There are also specific organizations, both local and national, that offer groups for particular types of bereavement, including groups for bereaved parents, people grieving a substance-related loss, and survivors of a suicide death.

③

Look for grief centers.

Grief centers are typically focused on bereaved children and families. They usually offer workshops, groups, and camps specifically for children. To see if there's one in your area, visit the website for the National Alliance for Children's Grief (childrengrieve.org) and check their "Find Support" section for camps and centers listed by state.

Look for meetups.

Keep an eye out for less formal types of groups that offer support around your loss. For example, there are happy hours for divorced parents and groups that meet over dinner to discuss death and grief. What's available in a particular area can vary, so search online or ask someone in your support system for a recommendation.

OTHER LISTS TO CHECK OUT:

5 Ws to Help You Understand Support Systems, page 51

3 To-Dos for Utilizing Your Support System, page 230

27 Things to Help You Feel Less Isolated, page 249

4

Reasons to Love the Concept of Continuing Bonds

Continuing bonds is kind of an "a-ha" grief concept. As in . . .

"A-ha! That makes so much sense."
"A-ha! I knew I wasn't crazy."
"A-ha! That's exactly how I feel."

Continuing bonds is an idea that brings clarity, normalcy, and understanding to many who hear it. It's a concept that makes so much sense it feels like you already knew it, except you didn't know that you knew it until someone put it into words.

The term was first described in the 1996 book *Continuing Bonds: New Understandings of Grief* edited by Dennis Klass, Phyllis Silverman, and Steven Nickman. In their respective works, the editors had observed many cases in which remaining connected to deceased loved ones provided people comfort and support in coping with loss and adjustment. This observation questioned existing paradigms that suggested healthy grief should lead to a place of detachment. Instead, the editors proposed that it is normal and often comforting for the bereaved to maintain their connection, or continue having bonds, with deceased loved ones.

We think this is a fundamental concept for those grieving the death of a loved one. However, if your loss is not death related, we still encourage you to read this list and consider how it might apply to your experiences. In some ways, continuing bonds could be relevant to any loss in which a loved one is absent or missed.

①

Continuing bonds acknowledges that grief is ongoing.

We've run out of metaphors for saying that grief never ends, so we'll just say it—grief never ends. It isn't something you *go through*; it's something that becomes a part of you. Especially if you're grieving a loved one.

②

Continuing bonds says it's normal to stay connected with your loved one.

Continuing bonds supports the idea that we carry deceased loved ones with us, often for our entire lives; we don't detach from them or leave them behind. Unfortunately, this validation isn't always found in our broader society or even in our own beliefs and attitudes about grief and coping.

③

Continuing bonds may describe many of your grief-related behaviors.

Holding on to items, daily habits, private rituals, conversations with your loved one, visiting places where you feel close to them, thinking about them—these are all ways people continue bonds with deceased loved ones. Though these behaviors may have been seen as pathological by older grief models, the theory of continuing bonds says they are entirely normal.

④

Continuing bonds says that not only are these behaviors normal, but they may help you cope with grief.

Because many people still believe that staying attached to a deceased loved one is pathological, some may worry about their continuing bonds and wonder, *Is this okay? Does this mean I'm not coping well with grief? Should I be worried? Am I stuck?* Fear not. Klass and his colleagues found in their research that, in many circumstances, remaining connected seemed to facilitate the bereaved's ability to cope with loss and accompanying life changes.

Of course, it's necessary to note that there are instances where continuing a bond with a deceased loved one is not healing. Just as relationships with the living can be complicated, so can relationships with the dead. If the relationship was troubling before the death, it might remain so afterward.

OTHER LISTS TO CHECK OUT:

5 FAQs About Yearning, page 91

20 Ways to Connect with Memories, page 268

11 Questions to Ask Yourself as You Begin to Move Forward, page 276

64

Tips for Surviving Holidays (and Other Special Days) After Loss

After a loss, grievers often find themselves in a terrible predicament. Tradition brings the contrast of then versus now into vivid clarity. You may think, "If only I could keep things the same . . ." or "Maybe we can pretend everything is fine . . ." or "If only my love one were still here . . ."

Unfortunately, things cannot remain the same, and it's important to acknowledge the loss and grief inherent in this reality. The worst thing you can do is head into your holiday ignoring the elephant in the room and crossing your fingers that things will work themselves out.

While we strongly encourage you to adjust your holiday plans in a way that's reflective of you and your family, this list may help you get your wheels turning about coping with tradition, holidays, and special days after a loss.

1. Acknowledge that elements of the day will be difficult.

2. Believe that parts of the day will be painful, but you will get through it.

3. Don't feel guilty for feeling grief on a day of celebration. It's normal and natural for days of celebration, happiness, and gratitude to also remind you of loss.

4. Allow for the possibility that you'll experience moments of joy and peace.

what's your grief?

5. Remember, small rituals are just as important as more significant traditions. We say this to reassure you that even if larger traditions have to change, keeping smaller and more doable traditions may provide a sense of consistency and comfort.

6. Know that tradition doesn't have to be perfect.

7. If you're grieving a loved one, creating a new tradition in their honor provides you an opportunity to find meaningful and lasting ways to remember them.

8. Change is okay, and it doesn't have to be forever. Family rituals and traditions are constantly adapting and evolving. This is normal.

9. Focus on the things you can control, and try not to get caught up in the things you can't.

10. To the extent that you can, plan ahead for how you will spend the day. Where will you go? Who will you spend it with? What will you do?

11. Include kids in planning the holidays. Let them tell you what's important to them and what they'd like to do. Be honest with them about things that might have to change. Most importantly, give them permission to enjoy themselves.

12. Be honest with yourself and others about what you do and don't want to do for the holiday.

13. Communicate with those you will be spending the day with. Is everyone in agreement about the plan? If specific roles need to be filled or traditions need to be carried out, who will step in?

14. If you will be spending the day with multiple grieving people, start a dialogue about how you will support each other. What elements of the day or holiday are people concerned about? What extra support do people think they'll need?

15. If you're spending the day alone, what will you do? A day of sulking? A day of self-care? A day of movies and jigsaw puzzles?

16. Think ahead about potential grief triggers and make a general plan for how you will cope when they crop up.

17. Push yourself to stick out the important parts of the day, but have a plan for how you will duck out or get some space if things start to feel overwhelming.

18. Though others may be grieving, remember not everyone will want to express their grief in the same way (or at all).

19. Acknowledge that others may decide to spend the holiday differently (i.e., by themselves). Though disappointing, this choice may be indicative of their unique grief needs.

20. Plan to check in with a friend, counselor, or grief support group before or after the day.

21. Send a holiday card to friends you've lost touch with.

22. Reach out to someone else you know who's struggling during this time of year.

23. If it's a milestone day for you or someone you love (graduation, wedding), think about, share, or ask for a piece of advice a loved one from your past would have given.

24. Pull out your coping bucket list from page 185 and highlight the coping that might be most helpful on the day.

25. Say no to extra events or obligations around the day if you're already feeling stressed.

26. Don't feel guilty saying no.

27. Don't carpool when attending an event that could become overwhelming (unless your friend agrees to leave when you're ready). You don't want to get stuck.

28. Set out old photo albums at your holiday gathering so people can reminisce.

29. Include family recipes or favorite dishes in the holiday meal.

30. Plan to have a smaller gathering than usual.

31. Plan to have a larger gathering than usual and invite old friends and long-distance family members.

32. Don't send holiday cards this year if it feels overwhelming (and let go of any guilt about it).

33. Talk as a family and decide whether you genuinely want (and can afford) to exchange gifts among adults.

34. Attend a gathering, workshop, or webinar for people grieving over the holiday.

35. Skip the decorations if they are too much. However, if you still want to feel festive, drive or walk around your neighborhood or an area where there are lots of decorations.

36. Log off of social media if happy holiday posts from your friends and family are making you miserable.

37. It's okay to cry in the middle of the day or celebration. It's also okay not to cry.

38. Ignore people who tell you what you should do for the holiday. Trust your gut.

39. If you find yourself slipping into a funk, take a minute to identify three things you feel grateful for.

40. Be mindful of your alcohol use around the holidays. Sometimes when you're feeling stressed, lonely, or awkward at the holiday party, one drink can turn into five.

41. If you want to avoid crowds, do your shopping online.

42. Splurge on a gift for yourself.

43. Ask for help.

44. Say yes to help.

45. Surround yourself with supportive people and grief friends.

46. Make quiet time for yourself or time to engage in well-being coping.

47. Take an hour to get organized if you're feeling overwhelmed by dates and to-dos.

48. If it would make your life easier to skip certain things, skip them if you can.

49. If it's an annual holiday, remember that next year will be different.

50. Give yourself permission to experience moments of joy, happiness, laughter, and peace.

If you're grieving a loved one's absence:

51. Light a candle in your home in memory of the person

52. Create a memory box (or stocking, basket, etc.). Ask people you're sharing the day with to write down memories and place them in the box. Pick a time to share them together.

53. Make a donation in your loved one's name to a charity that was important to them.

54. Buy a gift you would have given your loved one. Donate it to a local charity or give it to someone else.

55. Pick a few special items that belonged to your loved one and give them to friends or family members as gifts.

56. Make a memorial ornament, wreath, tree, or other decoration in honor of your loved one.

57. If you've been having a hard time parting with your loved one's things, use the holidays as an opportunity to donate items to people in need.

58. Visit a place where you feel close to your loved one and leave a wreath, flower, or another meaningful item.

59. Make a party or holiday playlist with your loved one's favorite music.

60. Leave an empty seat at the holiday table in memory of your loved one.

61. Volunteer in your loved one's memory.

62. Support grieving children by doing a remembrance grief activity or attending a family holiday workshop at a local grief center.

63. Donate flowers or other holiday decorations at your place of worship in memory of your loved one.

64. Observe a moment of silence during your holiday prayer or toast in memory of your loved one.

OTHER LISTS TO CHECK OUT:

Make Your Own List: What's Your Grief Trigger?, page 210
5 Building Blocks of Well-Being, page 182
4 Reasons to Love the Concept of Continuing Bonds, page 259

20

Ways to Connect
with Memories

We probably don't have to tell you that one of the saddest things about life after loss is that, with time, memories like the sound of a loved one's voice or the smell of your grandma's kitchen start to fade. Indeed, many grieving people have shared with us that the inability to access specific memories of people, places, and moments in the past is a troubling secondary loss. When you're really yearning to remember the past, these are some ways you may be able to connect with memories.

1. Look at photo albums or old photos.

2. Watch old videos.

3. Ask friends and family if they have any photos or albums you could look through.

4. Ask friends and family if they have photos they could post online or email to you.

5. Tell stories about the past.

6. Write or journal about the past.

7. Visit a place you haven't been to in a long time (your old hometown, high school, old house, etc.).

8. Learn more about your family history.

9. Construct your family tree.

10. Make a playlist of songs you used to listen to when you were younger.

11. Ask friends and family members to share stories of you when you were younger or stories of loved ones who have died.

12. Stop and notice when something you do is inspired by a loved one from the past, like a habit or a phrase you always say.

13. Display objects from people and places of the past around your home.

14. Keep your family traditions going. These can be significant holiday traditions or small traditions, like singing the same lullaby to your children that your grandmother used to sing to you.

15. Reconnect with someone you haven't spoken with in a long time.

16. Look at old yearbooks.

17. Cook recipes that remind you of your loved ones or the past.

18. Get back into an old hobby.

19. Reread books or rewatch television shows or movies that remind you of the past.

20. Share memories of the past with younger generations (ignore the eye rolls, they're more interested than they let on).

OTHER LISTS TO CHECK OUT:

5 FAQs About Yearning, page 91

5 Reasons It Can Feel Like Your Grief Has Been Forgotten, page 142

16 Questions to Help You Understand Your Grief Story, page 282

4

Facts to Remember When Life Doesn't Turn Out the Way You Planned

"What do you want to be when you grow up?" It is the question asked of all children starting at an age when they only know of about ten possibilities. But from that moment, we ask them to create a future in their minds. We ask them to imagine what life will look like—who they will be, what job they will have, where they will live. The very act of asking the question, harmless as it seems, suggests that they should know the answer, create a map to their destination, and be ever working toward it.

Then life does what life does. It unfolds with little regard for the life that we hoped for. Whether you lost a career, a home, your health, your hope for children, or a person who you always imagined would be part of your life, you're left facing the reality that the life you planned is no longer the life you will live. The map you created feels useless.

Feeling like the life you imagined is gone, confusion and overwhelm can quickly turn into an abyss of hopelessness and despair. For those moments, we have always found comfort in the words of Viktor Frankl, a Holocaust survivor and psychiatrist who said, "Everything can be taken from a man but one thing: the last of the human freedoms—to choose one's attitude in any given set of circumstances, to choose one's one way."

There is no perfect, sage wisdom for the moments when it feels that everything has been taken, that the map you created was for a life you can no longer live. But your ability to choose your own way remains, and that, coupled with the four following facts, can help with moving forward.

① Life never turns out *exactly* the way you planned.

Were you looking for something more hopeful? We're sorry. But this is an important truth. This loss might be the largest and most devastating you've experienced, but chances are it is not the first time life has not turned out as you planned. Though past losses may have seemed less significant, you likely struggled, to some extent, to imagine meaning in an uncertain future. In those instances, you survived and slowly your life grew around and forward from that loss. Hard as it is to imagine, that can happen again.

② The life you always imagined is not the only life worth living.

Though there is hope in this truth, we've also found it one of the hardest things to accept in grief. When you've always envisioned a particular life, conceived of all the ways you would find joy, purpose, and meaning in that life, it can feel like the only path. It can help to think of people you know are on very different paths than your own, people you know whose life paths had to change, or other paths you once considered—even if long, long ago.

(3)
Many things have had to change, but some things have come with you.

When your life has been turned upside down and the future you imagined is not the future you will live, it's common to focus on all that is lost. You can get bogged down in who you won't be, who you won't have, what you won't do, where you won't go. But there are pieces of you that are still you, people who are still with you, and values that still guide you. Although these don't diminish the loss, it is important to remember that you still have them.

(4)
You can yearn for the life you wanted while appreciating the life you have.

Finding gratitude and meaning in the life you're living following your loss does not diminish your grief. It doesn't make your loss any less devastating, and it certainly doesn't mean you're glad your loss happened. It simply means that as human beings, we are incredibly lucky to be able to wish for a life we were not able to have while at the same time appreciating the life we do have. They can exist side by side.

OTHER LISTS TO CHECK OUT:

Make Your Own List: What's Your Hope?, page 286

4 Things You Can Do to Cope with Conflicting Emotions, page 193

Make Your Own List: What's Your Identity? (A Before-and-After List), page 151

What's Your Reasons to Live List?

In 2017 the long-time radio show host of *Fresh Air*, Terry Gross, interviewed the author David Sedaris. He had recently released a book composed of curated entries from journals he kept from 1977 to 2002. She asked him to read a particular entry:

February 16, 1988, Chicago

Reasons to Stay Alive
- *Christmas*
- *The family beach trip*
- *Writing a published book*
- *Seeing my name in a magazine*
- *Watching C. grow bald*
- *Ronnie Ruedrich*
- *Seeing Amy [his sister] on TV*
- *Other people's books*
- *Outliving my enemies*
- *Being interviewed by Terry Gross on* Fresh Air

After reading the list aloud, a list written six years before the publication of Sedaris's first book and long before being interviewed on *Fresh Air*, Gross expressed being both flattered and concerned. She said it "made me worried because the headline on that entry is 'reasons to stay alive.' And I really didn't know how to interpret that. Was that, like, oh, things to look forward to in life, or did it mean reasons not to kill yourself?"

Sedaris responded, "It was reasons not to kill myself . . . I had broken up with somebody. And I was, you know, really upset and depressed. And so that was . . . reasons to keep going."

Gross's question is rooted in that problematic either/or thinking we referenced on page 193. It suggests that the options are either you want to live or you want to kill yourself. And this is no fault to Terry Gross. She's using the language we hear often in mental health: "Are you having thoughts of suicide?" "Have you had thoughts of harming yourself?" Yes or no?

For some, the answer is very clear. According to a 2020 study by the Substance Abuse and Mental Health Services Administration of the US Department of Health and Human Services, twelve million people have serious thoughts of suicide each year. That number grows when you look at people struggling with certain types of grief. For others grieving, the loss has been devastating but it has never once impacted their desire to live. And for many, the answer isn't clear at all.

If you've waded through the murky waters of illness, injury, trauma, loss, grief, or depression, perhaps you've been somewhere in the shades of gray, where the answer isn't yes or no. It sounds more like, "I haven't, but I have thought that it would be easier if I just didn't wake up tomorrow." Or, "No, I've never thought of suicide. I would never hurt myself, but I also don't have any desire to live any longer." And this answer can shift and turn from hour to hour.

Everyone should have a Reasons to Live list, wherever you fall on this nuanced spectrum. Call it whatever you like—reasons to wake up in the morning, things to look forward to, reasons not to kill yourself, things to be grateful for, things worth living for, reasons to keep going. Just remember that this is not a list meant to override your pain. It won't counteract your suffering. It is not meant to minimize the reality that putting one foot in front of the other can feel impossible some days.

As the philosopher Seneca said, "Sometimes even to live is an act of courage." This is your list to remind you why living is worth trying.

So here's what we want you to do:

- Grab a piece of paper and write down your reasons to live.

- When you're done, take a picture of the list and keep it on your phone. You never know when reading the reminder might be just what you need.

If You're Thinking of Suicide

Though not caring about life, not wanting to be alive, and wanting to die are all far more common than people realize, many nonetheless feel deeply ashamed admitting these thoughts. Many people have internalized the idea that having these thoughts is a sign of weakness or failure. They're not. If you're thinking of harming yourself in any way, please get help right away with the knowledge that there is no shame in any of your thoughts and feelings. Talking to someone can be incredibly helpful in easing your pain and thoughts of self-harm. If you don't have a therapist to talk to, you can contact the National Suicide Prevention Lifeline by phone at 800-273-TALK (8255) or by online chat at www.suicidepreventionlifeline.org.

11

Questions to Ask Yourself as You Begin to Move Forward

There is anecdotal wisdom that, whenever possible, you should wait six months to year after a significant loss to make a big life decision. If your goal is not to make any decisions until your "grief brain" has settled down a bit, that isn't bad advice. It rarely hurts to sleep on big decisions if you have that luxury to do so, because when your emotional state has altered significantly, it is hard to predict how you will feel later. George Loewenstein, a psychologist at Carnegie Mellon University, coined this challenge the "hot-cold empathy gap."

The empathy gap, which is well researched, says that when people are in a calm and nonthreatened state (a cold state), they have a hard time predicting how they would feel and act if they were feeling anger, fear, or even love (which are hot states), and vice versa. When people are anxious it's difficult to imagine being at ease; when you're experiencing the complicated emotions of acute grief, it's difficult to imagine a life beyond acute grief (Loewenstein, 2005).

But there are plenty of instances where waiting for calm skies before making a big decision just isn't realistic. Or you may not be interested in waiting. In any of these cases, ask yourself these clarifying questions before making a big decision soon after a loss.

1. Do I need to make this decision now, or can I wait a little bit longer?

2. Do I *want* to make this decision now, knowing my mindset might look quite different in a few months?

3. Is this decision coming from a place of avoidance? Am I trying to escape a person, place, or thing that is a reminder of my loss?

4. If so, can I work on getting comfortable with my own pain to prevent me from making a big decision exclusively to avoid it?

5. Is this an incredibly big risk that I'm taking because I am worried that life is short?

6. Will I be able to cope with the physical/emotional/financial/relational/spiritual fallout if things don't go the way I imagine in the short term? In the long term?

7. Will this decision hurt people I love? If so, who? Can I live with that hurt? Have I talked with that person? Is this decision worth damaging or losing this relationship?

8. Was this something I ever wanted or considered before my loss?

9. What are the risks of postponing this decision?

10. Which of my values are supported by this decision? Which of my values are violated by this decision?

11. If someone I loved dearly were considering this decision, what question would I ask them? What advice would I give them?

OTHER LISTS TO CHECK OUT:

7 Steps to Help You Live According to Your Values, page 167

6 Ways Grief Can Change Your Priorities, page 145

3 Existential Questions Prompted by Loss, page 148

5

Areas of Post-Loss Growth

"And once the storm is over you won't remember how you made it through, how you managed to survive. You won't even be sure, in fact, whether the storm is really over. But one thing is certain. When you come out of the storm you won't be the same person who walked in. That's what this storm's all about."

—HARUKI MURAKAMI, *KAFKA ON THE SHORE*

There's a notion out there, particularly on social media and in some self-help resources, that suggests that, with the proper perspective, a person's grief will become a vehicle for transformation, renewal, self-discovery, or metamorphosis. The myth here is not that these outcomes can happen—because they can—but that one should expect them to. Or that one has failed at grief if they don't eventually reach a place where they feel they've grown and become better than before.

Here's the truth of the matter: growth is not the goal of grieving. Nor is it a mark that someone has grieved well. Grieving is the process of survival, resilience, rebuilding, connecting with the past, redefining

what's your grief?

your identity, recalibrating your values, and so on. Some people will experience growth as a by-product of this process, but certainly not all. And, those who do feel they've experienced growth often don't see it this way for some time after their loss.

Another little-known truth is that one may feel they have experienced growth in their grief yet still feel intense pain over the loss. It's important to talk about the true nature of post-traumatic growth (PTG) so people understand that it's not an easy path out of or around pain. On the contrary, only through confronting and struggling with pain can such growth and transformation occur. In fact, the researcher who first observed and studied this type of growth, Richard Tedeschi, is careful to clarify, "Post-traumatic growth is not happiness . . . it often coexists with distress" (Sarner, 2021).

So what exactly is post-traumatic growth? Prominent PTG researchers Richard Tedeschi and Lawrence Calhoun define posttraumatic growth as "positive psychological change experienced as a result of the struggle with highly challenging life circumstances."

It's important to draw the distinction between resilience and PTG. Resilience typically refers to an ability to withstand hardship and remain psychologically healthy despite adversity. With PTG, a person's worldview has been so shattered that they cannot not experience resilience. They have not remained psychologically healthy and could not move forward in any direction. But through (and only through) their struggle and rebuilding, they experience growth.

For our purposes in this list, it doesn't really matter if you've experienced resilience, PTG, or you're just busy wading through the muck and couldn't be less interested in labels like these. All we want you to know is that there are five areas where growth commonly occurs. Sometimes it is post-traumatic growth; sometimes it is making meaning from your loss. Whether or not you feel growth in these areas is not a measure of success or failure. But knowing them may help you observe and approach your grief from a place of curiosity.

(1) Greater appreciation for life and/or changed sense of priorities

Growth in this area might mean you . . .

- Have a greater sense of appreciation for what you have
- Experience a shift in priorities
- Redefine what you consider important
- Have a greater appreciation for the small things in life

(2) Openness to new possibilities in life

Often the realization of vulnerability and the discovery of new strength and perspective can lead people to make new or more meaningful decisions regarding their life's path.

(3) More intimate, deeper, or warmer relationships with others

We'll admit that we focus a lot on the bad and the ugly of support systems after a loss, but the truth is that many people have wonderful grief-related personal interactions. You might experience growth in this area if you . . .

- Feel a greater sense of compassion for others
- Experience compassion from others
- Are able to focus on the relationships that truly matter and ignore those that are harmful or unhelpful

- Feel the experience has helped you to find out who your friends are
- Realize the need to cherish your relationships

(4)
Spiritual growth

Whether you fancied yourself a religious person at the time of the trauma or not, struggling with existential and spiritual questions can often lead to a deeper, more refined sense of belief and understanding. The growth comes through the grappling.

(5)
A sense of increased (or discovered) personal strength

Many people have the sense that if they've survived their loss, they handle anything. Growth in this area might be experienced as . . .

- A greater sense of self-control and emotional balance
- An enhanced ability to cope and adapt
- A greater sense of perspective during times of hardship
- Increased feelings of independence and confidence

OTHER LISTS TO CHECK OUT:

6 Ways Grief Can Change Your Priorities, page 145

3 Existential Questions Prompted by Loss, page 148

Make Your Own List: What's Your Identity? (A Before-and-After List), page 151

16

Questions to Help You Understand Your Grief Story

> *"To live is to suffer, to survive is to find meaning in the suffering."*
>
> — GORDON ALLPORT

There are billions of moments that have made up your big, beautiful, ugly, messy, complicated life.

These moments have shaped the narrative you tell about what you've done, where you've been, what you believe, whom you love, what you are doing, where you are going, what's mattered, what hasn't, what you hope for, what you fear, how you've succeeded, when you have failed, and who you are. Whatever the loss that brought you to this book, it crashed into your life, and chances are you're still making sense of what it means for you and your story.

After a significant loss, it's tempting to live life in the past—wishing it had been different, screaming that it was unfair; deconstructing every decision to figure out where things went wrong or what you could have done differently, imagining what life would be like now had the past turned out the way you wish it had. But as the existential psychologist Irving Yalom said, sooner or later we all have to "give up the hope for a better past."

You cannot change the facts of your history; you cannot change your loss. But you can integrate that loss into who you are now and decide what that will mean for you as you move forward. It is easy to conceptualize life as a series of events that happen to you, and your story as the reporting of those events. But it is not that simple. It is not just what has happened to you that shapes you. The way that you make sense of what has happened to you also shapes you.

There is the story you have lived up until this moment and then there is the story you are still living, telling, and creating. You are not just the storyteller; you are the story writer. How you understand the story of your past and your present is shaping a future that is still unfolding.

Your grief story is yours to write, there is no single list of questions that will allow you to make sense of your past and determine the meaning it will bring to your future. That will be a process that will always continue and evolve. Now, decades after some of our own earliest losses, we both continue to revisit them, re-grieve them, and understand their role and meaning in our lives in different ways. Your grief story never ends because your loss is woven into who you are and your life that continues to grow.

These questions are a place to start understanding your story. Use them or don't. Add to the list. Revisit them every few months or few years.

1. Who were you before your loss?

2. Who are you now?

3. What did you lose?

4. What did you believe about yourself before the loss that you no longer believe?

5. What do you believe about yourself now that you did not believe before?

6. What did you believe about other people before the loss that you no longer believe?

7. What do you believe about other people now that you did not believe before?

8. What did you believe about the world before the loss that you no longer believe?

9. What do you believe about the world now that you did not believe before?

10. What was important to you before your loss that is not important to you now?

11. What is important to you now that was not important to you before?

12. Knowing what you know now, if you could go back to the time when the loss happened, what would you tell yourself?

13. What has this loss given you or taught you?

14. What has this loss taken from you that you did not expect?

15. Has your loss brought new meaning or new growth to your life?

16. When you look back on your loss in ten years, how do you hope it will have impacted your life?

What's Your Hope?

People often mistake hope as something that can only come after grief, but that doesn't make sense if you think about it. Hope must exist alongside grief because without the darkness, why would you ever wish for light? Hope exists because you're lost in suffering, and before you find the path out, you must have hope that you'll find it.

Of course, there are times when you feel like you've lost all hope. Feeling hopeless is common in grief and, frankly, makes sense when you consider that hope means to wish for something with the anticipation and expectation of fulfilling that desire. The question becomes, do you believe you can reliably anticipate your hopes to be fulfilled? Because loss teaches you to be careful with your expectations and desires. And when you start to doubt that you'll have the things you want or need, you may begin to feel hopeless.

But hope is never gone entirely. It's always there when you're ready for it. And because you've opened this book and made it to the end, we're going to go out on a limb and assume you are ready. That said, hope may be hard to spot because, for many people, it looks different than they pictured. In the context of grief, it is not a fluffy, happy kind of hope. It's not something that lifts you up and transports you over your troubles. Instead, hope after loss is gritty, resilient. The kind of hope that stands its ground in the face of extreme uncertainty and doubt. The kind of hope that knows where you've been, knows what it's up against, knows when to stay silent, and knows when to quietly whisper, "Maybe."

Our most fervent wish is for you to move forward with hope. Whether your hopes are big or small, if you can imagine feeling better in the future, then that's hopeful. But, of course, we know you may not know what you hope for anymore. You have changed—your life, relationships, and future have changed—so your hopes and dreams have naturally changed as well.

So here's what we want you to do:

- Get out a piece of paper and a pen. Write "I hope . . ." and then finish the sentence.

- Do this over and over again.

- Add things big and small.

- Add things that would make your life feel more livable.

- Add things that align with your values.

- Add things that might make you feel joy, comfort, connection, love, or peace.

- Do this until you can't think of anything else to add.

Bibliography

Barlow, D. H. *Anxiety and Its Disorders: The Nature and Treatment of Anxiety and Panic.* New York: Guilford Press, 1988.

Bonanno, G. A. *The Other Side of Sadness: What the New Science of Bereavement Tells Us About Life After Loss.* New York: Basic Books, 2010.

Boss, P. *Loss, Trauma, and Resilience: Therapeutic Work with Ambiguous Loss.* New York: W. W. Norton, 2006.

Bowlby, J., and C. M. Parkes. "Separation and Loss within the Family." In *The Child in His Family: International Yearbook of Child Psychiatry and Allied Professions*, edited by E. J. Anthony and C. Koupernik, 197–216. New York: Wiley, 1970.

Brown, B. "Shame Resilience Theory: A Grounded Theory Study on Women and Shame." *Families in Society* 87, no. 1 (January 2006): 43–52. https://doi.org/10.1606/1044-3894.3483.

Bruce, E., and C. Schultz. "Non-finite Loss and Challenges to Communication Between Parents and Professionals." *British Journal of Special Education* 29, no. 1 (March 2002).

Carroll, L. *Alice's Adventures in Wonderland.* Peterborough, ON: Broadview Press, 2000.

Center for Prolonged Grief website. Columbia University School of Social Work. Last modified April 27, 2021. https://prolongedgrief.columbia.edu/professionals/complicated-grief-professionals/overview.

Corrigan, P. W., and D. Rao. "On the Self-Stigma of Mental Illness: Stages, Disclosure, and Strategies for Change." *Canadian Journal of Psychiatry* 57, no. 8 (2012): 464–69. https://doi.org/10.1177/070674371205700804.

Didion, J. *The Year of Magical Thinking.* New York: A. A. Knopf, 2006.

Doka, K. J. *Disenfranchised Grief: New Directions, Challenges, and Strategies for Practice.* Champaign, IL: Research Press, 2002.

Eisma, M. C., M. S. Stroebe, H. A. W. Schut, J. van den Bout, P. A. Boelen, and W. Stroebe. "Development and Psychometric Evaluation of the Utrecht Grief Rumination Scale." *Journal of Psychopathology and Behavioral Assessment* 36, no. 1 (2014): 165–76.

Eisma, M. C., M. S. Stroebe, H. A. W. Schut, W. Stroebe, P. A. Boelen, and J. van den Bout. "Avoidance Processes Mediate the Relationship Between Rumination and Symptoms of Complicated Grief and Depression Following Loss." *Journal of Abnormal Psychology* 122, no. 4 (2013): 961–70.

Frankl, V. E. *Man's Search for Meaning: An Introduction to Logotherapy.* Boston: Beacon Press, 1962.

Freud, S. "The Neuro-Psychoses of Defence (1894)." In *The Standard Edition of the Complete Psychological Works of Sigmund Freud*, Vol. 3, 41–61. New York: Vintage Classics, 2001.

———. *On Murder, Mourning and Melancholia.* London: Penguin Books, 2005.

Grimm, J., and W. Grimm. "Sehnsucht." *Deutsches Wörterbuch.* Munich: Deutscher Taschen-buchverlag, 1984. Reprinted from *German Dictionary* by J. Grimm and W. Grimm, Leipzig: Hirzel, 1854–1871.

Hayes, S. C. *Get Out of Your Mind and Into Your Life: The New Acceptance and Commitment Therapy.* Oakland: New Harbinger Publications, 2005.

Hibberd, R., L. S. Elwood, and T. E. Galovski. "Risk and Protective Factors for Posttraumatic Stress Disorder, Prolonged Grief, and Depression in Survivors of the Violent Death of a Loved One." *Journal of Loss and Trauma* 15, no. 5 (2010): 426–47. https://doi.org/10.1080/15325024.2010.507660.

Holt-Lunstad, J. "Social Isolation and Health." *Health Affairs.* June 21, 2020. https://www.healthaffairs.org/do/10.1377/hpb20200622.253235/full.

Holt-Lunstad, J., T. B. Smith, M. Baker, T. Harris, and D. Stephenson. "Loneliness and Social Isolation as Risk Factors for Mortality: A Meta-analytic Review." *Perspectives on Psychological Science* 10, no. 2 (2015): 227–37.

Kierkegaard, S. *Fear and Trembling: Dialectical Lyric by Johannes de Silentio.* Translated by A. Hannay. London: Penguin Classics, 1985.

Klass, D., P. R. Silverman, and S. L. Nickman. *Continuing Bonds: New Understandings of Grief.* Washington, DC: Taylor and Francis, 1996.

Klass, D., and E. Steffen. *Continuing Bonds in Bereavement: New Directions for Research and Practice*. New York: Routledge, Taylor & Francis Group, 2018.

Kray, L. J., L. G. George, K. A. Liljenquist, A. D. Galinsky, P. E. Tetlock, and N. J. Roese. "From What Might Have Been to What Must Have Been: Counterfactual Thinking Creates Meaning." *Journal of Personality and Social Psychology* 98, no. 1 (January 2010): 106–18. https://doi.org/10.1037/a0017905.

Kubler-Ross, E. *On Death and Dying: What the Dying Have to Teach Doctors, Nurses, Clergy and Their Own Families*. New York: Scribner, 2014.

Kubler-Ross, E., and D. Kessler. *On Grief and Grieving: Finding the Meaning of Grief through the Five Stages of Loss*. London: Simon & Schuster, 2014.

Lazarus, R. S., and S. Folkman. *Stress, Appraisal, and Coping*. New York: Springer, 1984.

Lewis, C. S. *A Grief Observed*. London: Faber & Faber, 1968.

Lindemann, E. "Symptomatology and Management of Acute Grief." Originally published 1944. *American Journal of Psychiatry* 151, no. 6 suppl (1994), 155–60.

Maciejewski, P. K., B. Zhang, S. D. Block, and H. G. Prigerson. "An Empirical Examination of the Stage Theory of Grief." *JAMA* 297, no. 7 (February 21, 2007): 716–23. https://doi.org/10.1001/jama.297.7.716.

Mezzacappa, E. S. "Epinephrine, Arousal, and Emotion: A New Look at Two-Factor Theory." *Cognition & Emotion* 13, no. 2 (1999): 181–99.

Neal, D. T., W. Wood, and J. M. Quinn. "Habits—A Repeat Performance." *Current Directions in Psychological Science* 15, no. 4 (2006): 198–202.

Newman, M. G., and S. J. Llera. "A Novel Theory of Experiential Avoidance in Generalized Anxiety Disorder: A Review and Synthesis of Research Supporting a Contrast Avoidance Model of Worry." *Clinical Psychology Review* 31, no. 3 (April 2011): 371–82. https://doi.org/10.1016/j.cpr.2011.01.008.

Nolen-Hoeksema, S., B. E. Wisco, and S. Lyubomirsky. "Rethinking Rumination." *Perspectives on Psychological Science* 3, no. 5 (2008): 400–424.

Norton, M. I., and F. Gino. "Rituals Alleviate Grieving for Loved Ones, Lovers, and Lotteries." *Journal of Experimental Psychology*: General 143, no. 1 (February 2014): 266–72. https://doi.org/10.1037/a0031772.

O'Connor, M.-F., and T. Sussman. "Developing the Yearning in Situations of Loss Scale: Convergent and Discriminant Validity for Bereavement, Romantic Breakup, and Homesickness." *Death Studies* 38: 450–58. https://doi.org/10.1080/07481187.2013.782928.

Oxford University Press. "Yearn". Lexico.com. 2021. https://www.lexico.com/en/definition/yearn.

Perlman, D., and Peplau, L. "Loneliness." In *Encyclopedia of Mental Health*, Vol. 2, edited by H. S. Friedman, 571–81. San Diego: Academic Press, 1998.

Rando, T. A. *How to Go on Living When Someone You Love Dies*. New York: Bantam Books, 1991.

———. *Treatment of Complicated Mourning*. Champaign, IL: Research Press, 1992.

Rubin, S. S. "The Two-Track Model of Bereavement: Overview, Retrospect, and Prospect." *Death Studies* 23, no. 8 (1999): 681–714.

Sarner, M. "Post-traumatic Growth: The Woman Who Learned to Live a Profoundly Good Life After Loss." *Guardian*. May 11, 2021. http://www.theguardian.com/lifeandstyle/2021/may/11/post-traumatic-growth-the-woman-who-learned-to-live-a-profoundly-good-life-after-loss.

Seligman, M. E. P. *Learned Optimism: How to Change Your Mind and Your Life*. New York: Vintage Books, 2006.

———. *Flourish: A Visionary New Understanding of Happiness and Well-Being*. New York: Atria Books, 2011.

Shear, M. K. "Complicated Grief." *New England Journal of Medicine* 372, no. 2 (2015): 153–60.

Smeets, E., K. Neff, H. Alberts, and M. Peters. "Meeting Suffering with Kindness: Effects of a Brief Self-Compassion Intervention for Female College Students." *Journal of Clinical Psychology* 70, no. 9 (September 2014): 794–807. https://doi.org/10.1002/jclp.22076.

Stroebe, M., and H. Schut. "The Dual Process Model of Coping with Bereavement: Rationale and Description." *Death Studies* 23, no. 3 (1999): 197–224.

Stroebe, M., P. A. Boelen, M. van den Hout, W. Stroebe, E. Salemink, and J. van den Bout. "Ruminative Coping as Avoidance: A Reinterpretation of Its

Function in Adjustment to Bereavement." *European Archives of Psychiatry and Clinical Neuroscience* 257, no. 8 (2007): 462–72.

Tedeschi, R. G., J. Shakespeare-Finch, K. Taku, and L. G. Calhoun. "Theories Related to Posttraumatic Growth." In *Posttraumatic Growth*, 60–80. New York: Routledge, 2018. https://doi.org/10.4324/9781315527451-8.

Tilghman-Osborne, C., D. A. Cole, and J. W. Felton. "Definition and Measurement of Guilt: Implications for Clinical Research and Practice." *Clinical Psychology Review* 30, no. 5 (2010): 536–46.

"2020 U.S. Report: Loneliness in the Workplace Survey." Cigna. Accessed September 9, 2021. https://www.cigna.com/static/www-cigna-com /docs/about-us/newsroom/studies-and-reports/combatting-loneliness /cigna-2020-loneliness-factsheet.pdf.

"Understanding the Stress Response." Harvard Health Publishing. July 6, 2020. https://www.health.harvard.edu/staying-healthy/understanding -the-stress-response.

VandenBos, G. *APA Dictionary of Psychology.* 2nd ed. Washington, DC: American Psychological Association, 2015.

Warren, F. "Tell Me a Secret." Reported by L. Cowan and produced by A. Shavelson. *Sunday Morning*, CBS, April 28, 2019. https://www.cbsnews.com/ news/postsecret-private-secrets-anonymously-shared-with-the-world.

Weiten, W., and D. McCann. *Psychology: Themes and Variations.* 7th ed. Toronto: Nelson, 2006.

Wood, W., J. M. Quinn, and D. A. Kashy. "Habits in Everyday Life: Thought, Emotion, and Action." *Journal of Personality and Social Psychology* 83, no. 6 (2002): 1281–97.

Worden, J. W. *Grief Counseling and Grief Therapy: A Handbook for the Mental Health Practitioner.* 5th ed. New York: Springer Publishing Company, 2018.

Yalom, I. D. *Existential Psychotherapy.* New York: Basic Books, 1980.

Zhou, X., T. Wildschut, C. Sedikides, X. Chen, and A. J. Vingerhoets. "Heartwarming Memories: Nostalgia Maintains Physiological Comfort." *Emotion* 12, no. 4 (August 2012): 678–84. https://doi.org/10.1037/a0027236.

The List of Lists

Part Three: Coping with Grief

Index

new possibilities, openness to, 280
Nickman, Steven, 38, 259–61
Nietzsche, Friedrich, 167
no, saying, 237
nondeath losses, obstacles to grieving, 45–47
nonfinite grief, 30
Norton, Michael, 90
nostalgia, 93. *See also* yearning
nothing, feeling, 99–100, 114. *See also* apathy
not-to-do list, 58–61
numbness, 99–100, 114

O'Connor, Mary-Frances, 91
off guard, fear of being caught, 86
optimistic griever, 56
others: cutting off support of, 140; reasons loss creates conflict with, 131–33. *See also* isolation; loneliness; support system(s)
out, venturing, 253
outlook, 153. *See also* worldview, disrupted

pace, going at your own, 204
pain: anger as sign of, 128; as connection to deceased, 157; statements bypassing, 109; and writing people off, 239
Parkes, Colin Murray, 35
past: sadness in leaving, 70; thinking about, 43, wanting to change, 71
Peplau, Letita Anne, 134
Perlman, Daniel, 134
permission to grieve, 139
personal strength, sense of increased, 281
pessimistic griever, 56
pets, 254
physical identity, 153
plans, unrealized, 270–72
poise, 112
post-traumatic growth (PTG), 278–81
post-traumatic stress, 76
pressure, as source of grief-related stress, 126
priorities, changed, 145–47, 280
process, grief as unpredictable, 20
procrastination, 82

professional identity, 152
progress, signs of, 162–66. *See also* growth, post-loss; moving forward
projection, 117
prolonged grief, 31–32
purpose, as impacted by loss, 50, 149

questions, existential, prompted by loss, 148–50

Rando, Therese, 36
Rao, Deepa, 105
rational coping, 180
rebuilding, 156, 161
regression, 117
regret: anger and dealing with, 128; versus guilt, 102; living with, 218–22
relational identity, 152
relational secondary losses, 39
relationships: as building block of well-being, 183; deepened, 280–81
relief, 72, 97–98
reminiscing, 93
resilience, 279
rituals, 90, 243
Rogers, Fred, 206
roles, changed, and conflict over loss, 133
Rubin, Simon, 37
rumination, 94–96, 103, 213–17. *See also* thoughts

Schut, Henk, 37, 96, 173–74
secondary losses, 39–41, 151–52
secret, grief, 110–11
Sedaris, David, 273
sehnsucht, 91
self-care, 204
self-forgiveness, finding, 223–27
selfishness, 147
self-kindness, 200–202, 205
selflessness, 147
self-stigma, 105–6
Seligman, Martin, 56, 182
Seneca, 274

Acknowledgments

A huge thanks to those without whom this book would never exist:

Eleanor's mom and Litsa's dad, who died before either of us got into this work. We're so grateful for the things that your lives and deaths taught us about life and loss, though we would certainly trade those lessons, our careers, and this book to have you back.

Our friends and family, who've supported us since the beginning of What's Your Grief. When we were a blog with twenty-five readers, you represented twenty of them. Whether you were humoring us, taking us seriously, or a little of both—you were there, and that meant everything.

The readers of the What's Your Grief site. You've been creating What's Your Grief along with us since the beginning. In the midst of your deepest pain, you've trusted us with your stories, encouraged us, shared our work, and supported one another. We're incredibly lucky to call so many of you *grief friends*.

The team at Quirk Books, who trusted us to write this book. Thank you for your dedication, hard work, and patience with us as we navigated the book writing process for the first time.

Our spouses, partners, and children who put up with us over the last year. You gracefully dealt with our distraction, angst, and self-doubt over writing this book. Thank you for your reassurance and for having more confidence in us than we had in ourselves. We love you.

About the Authors

Eleanor Haley, MS, and Litsa Williams, MA, LCSW-C, are the cofounders of the online grief community What's Your Grief. They are mental health professionals with a combined twenty-five-plus years of experience working with people coping with all types of complicated losses and life transitions.

Eleanor and Litsa met while supporting families who had lost loved ones to traumatic and unexpected deaths in Baltimore. They quickly bonded over their personal losses and their frustration finding grief resources that they would have used themselves or that they wanted to refer their clients to. After years of complaining, the two founded What's Your Grief as an online space with the simple goal of helping people better understand and cope with loss. They were willing to share their own losses (and confident that grief support is better without tilted heads and soothing tones), and their community organically grew to over five million visitors each year, quickly establishing itself as one of the largest and most trafficked grief support websites.

Eleanor holds a master's degree in counseling psychology from Loyola University of Maryland. Litsa received her master's degree in clinical social work from the University of Maryland School of Social Work and her master's in philosophy from the University of Warwick in the UK. Though much of the value in Eleanor and Litsa's work comes from their professional expertise, between the two they have lost parents in early adulthood and experienced the traumatic brain injury of a sibling, the substance use disorders of immediate family members, divorce, unexpected deaths of close friends, and the loss of a loved one to overdose. Their commitment to a book on coping with losses of all shapes and sizes runs far beyond the professional.